THE DAUGHTER OF JORIO

THE

DAUGHTER OF JORIO

A PASTORAL TRAGEDY

BY

GABRIELE D'ANNUNZIO

TRANSLATED FROM THE ITALIAN

BY

CHARLOTTE PORTER, PIETRO ISOLA
AND ALICE HENRY

WITH A PORTRAIT AND PICTURES FROM THE
ITALIAN PRODUCTION

GREENWOOD PRESS, PUBLISHERS
NEW YORK   1968

Printed in the United States of America

TO

THE LAND OF THE ABRUZZI, TO MY MOTHER

TO MY SISTERS, TO MY BROTHERS

ALSO

TO MY FATHER, ENTOMBED, TO ALL MY DEAD

AND TO ALL MY RACE BETWEEN THE

MOUNTAIN AND THE SEA

THIS SONG OF THE ANTIQUE BLOOD

I CONSECRATE

INTRODUCTION

AN elemental savor of the savage blood of the ancient race clings to the country of the Abruzzi. This elemental quality, intensely impressional and tragic, underlies the light sensitive beauty and bright artistic grace characteristic of Italy in general.

The lore and customs of the native folk, growing the vine and olive in the sunny slopes running seaward to the southern Adriatic, have been shut away from the easy touch of western Europe by the towering ridge of the Apennines, on whose rugged slopes the sheep are pastured. It is still the most archaic, the most stubbornly unmetropolitan corner of Italy. Here, even more than elsewhere in the country beloved of all other younger countries, the mediæval and the Pagan worlds linger intimately together, blending faiths and customs. It is a good soil and a fertile for growing an enduring masterpiece that shall gather Italy

INTRODUCTION

up into its being, and taste of the profound, immortal heart of the land.

In this land of the Abruzzi, and in the dim enchanted epoch of " once upon a time," " The Daughter of Jorio " is set. As the drama unfolds it carries with it this charmèd atmosphere. Who reads or hears this " song of the antique blood " is suddenly at home, too, in the Abruzzi, and catches the life along with the music of many years ago.

As descendants from the Abruzzi stock, two friends — D'Annunzio, the poet, and Michetti, the painter, travelled throughout their fatherland together, faring up the majestic snow-cloaked Maella and the precipitous Gran Sasso, to and fro among the rocky sheepsteads and caverns of the mountains, and along the bordering stretches of sea-shore.

They heard, then, a name, spoken in a way belonging to common custom there. Grown persons in this pastoral region are still known in patriarchal manner, not by their own names but merely as son or daughter of their father. The melody of the name thus heard haunted the memories of the artist-travellers. As the gipsy refrain Browning heard while a boy thrilled his blood like a call from the Wild —

INTRODUCTION

"Following the Queen of the Gipsies, O!" and bore poetic fruit long afterward in "The Flight of the Duchess," so, likewise, this sonorous name stirred the secret chords of artistic response in the imagination of these two friends and bore subconscious fruit in them. The fruit is different enough, yet of a kindred germ and flavor. Each has rendered it as a tribute to the mother-country in whose traditions he was cradled.

The name they heard — "La figlia di Jorio," meaning much to them, little to another, — may now be understood to be in itself eloquent of the old tribal feeling. This feeling, sinking the son in the father, places him apart from any other rule or influence than that of his own kith and kin. It admits no honorable union with one outside the clan without pang and social upheaval.

The mere name thus held within it, for the imaginative conception of genius, the seed of tragic social clash between alien castes or warring rival families. Such clash between warring Italian families Shakespeare showed in the love of a Capulet and a Montague. The imperative elemental drawing together of Juliet and her Romeo ran counter to long-

INTRODUCTION

established grooves of social cleavage. It was
a cleavage not to be welded except through the
woe and spiritual triumph of love. Such clash
between the established pastoral clan and the
outcast is the theme which slumbered in this
name for both D'Annunzio and Michetti.
D'Annunzio's development of it leads by a
different path to a triumph of love as spirit-
ually exalting and as socially significant as
Shakespeare's.

For Michetti, the haunting name resulted,
shortly after their journey, in some wonderful
pictures, — sketches in water-color for a great
painting in oil, now owned in Berlin, where it
gives lustre to the Geeger collection, — later
a large pastel exhibited in 1895, in the Inter-
national Exposition of the Fine Arts at Venice.

Michetti's imagination presented the daughter of Jorio as a wanderer, with a cloak covering her head and held shieldingly over the
breast by the right hand, while she passes a
group of staring rustics. Her long rushing
strides, as of one who " knows well the pathways," have a strangely alluring motion, like
that of a majestic hunted fugitive. One of
the five men whose gaze she attracts is riveted
by her look. To the others she means less than

nothing. She is an outcast or a laughing-stock. To this one she means a mystic appeal thrown into his life to stamp it forever.

Not until many years after the journey through the Abruzzi, in 1903, at Mettuno, the haunting name, fused with some germinal impression flowing from Michetti's pictures, resulted for D'Annunzio in his " La Figlia di Jorio." The plot is of his own pure imagination all compact. It rests upon no legend, he says. The creative idea came in a compelling influence that gripped him while busied in other absorbing poetic work belonging to a series he has had in mind, and involving historic research in the past of Italy. These annals of the Malatesta this sudden influence bade him put aside. It called him, instead, to pour himself out, with an ardor imperious and self-assured, in a glowing flood of strongly-stressed rhythmic poetry. The flood of fire took molten shape in this tragedy. It embodied not the historic life of warring nobles, but the obscure, toiling, pastoral life of antique Italy.

The result is a tragedy vividly spectacular, dramatically strong and simple. The picturesque loveliness belonging to the opening of each act is cut sharply across with the ruthless

INTRODUCTION

inrush of direct vital action. Into the graceful
beauty of the lyrical espousal scene of the first
Act is thrust the pitiless hunting down of Mila,
the daughter of Jorio, by the brutal barking
band of reapers. In the midst of the serene
idealism of the uplifted group in Aligi's meagre
mountain cave, where, in the second Act, love
and art and insight reinforce and befriend each
other, close, even, upon the sanctity of the kiss
of the kneeling lovers, is thrust the crass bestial
domination of the lusty Lazaro, equipped and
privileged to do his evil will. This, perforce,
leads to the lightning stroke of the murder.
Finally, in the third Act, the poetic veil of
meandering lament and tender commiseration
of the kindred for the stricken family is rent
away by the brusque entrance, the swift direct
speech, and decisive help of the daughter of
Jorio. The self-sacrifice of her ripened transcendent love is then the opportunity for con-
centrating against her the blind clamor of their
crude social justice. The final climax of contrasts is attained by these tumultuous voices
of the surging mob on the one side crying,
" To the fire, to the flames with the daughter
of Jorio!" and, on the other side, by the voice
of the clear-sighted Ornella calling in majesty,

INTRODUCTION

" Mila, Mila! My sister in Jesus, I kiss your
two feet that bear you away! Heaven is for
thee!" and the soaring, rapturous voice of
Mila, the outcast, who has taken all their sins
upon herself, and who cries, "The flame is
beautiful! The flame is beautiful!"

These clear-cut contrasts are masterly for
the stage either of the theatre or the human
breast. They strike to the quick of each char-
acter, to the core of the meaning of every situation. Throwing open each particular heart in
its degree to comprehension, they reveal it also
to sympathy. At the same time they cast upon
the social sanction of the evil domination of
Lazaro and upon the separate woes of all those
"who suffer and know not wherefore," the
larger light insensibly illumining the plot as
a whole and disclosing its typical relation to
the plot of life in general. Thus, in the emo-
tionalized manner possible only to genius at
mountain-peak moments, the play illumines
the perennial relations of a predestined love to
art and aspiration and of all three to social
life, which sacrifices all three when it wists not
what it does.

The vivid picturesqueness of such scenes as
those of the espousal rites, in the first Act; the

mourning of the kindred, and the folk-judgment of the third Act; the interesting figures of Malde, the treasure-seeker, the herb gatherer, and the wise old saint of the mountain of the second Act; in fact, the homely episodes of pastoral life throughout the drama rest upon traditional customs and rooted beliefs of the Abruzzi.

At Pratola, Peligna, and other places in the Abruzzi the mother-in-law receives her son's bride into her house with a nuptial ritual full of poetic symbolism, — a ritual independent of that of the Church. According to Antonio de Nino, — whose work on the "Habits and Customs of the Abruzzi" scientifically verifies the folk-lore D'Annunzio puts alive before us, — the mother breaks the bread, the symbol of fertility, over the son and the daughter. And as she touches the forehead, breast, and shoulders, she says: "May we live together like Christians and not like cats and dogs." She initiates her new daughter to her fireside by calling to her notice home-objects to which special virtue was attributed: the andiron-chain that could lull storms; the mortar that, if placed on the window-sill, lured back the stray pigeon; the salt, which if hung in a pouch around the baby's neck could keep it safe from the vampire.

The bride's kindred came to share in the ceremonial of espousal, as in the play, first gathering at the house of the mother, whom they always brought with them with honor at the close of their procession. To the new home they advanced in single file, bearing on their heads the *donora*, gifts of baskets of grain, with fluttering ribbons, and on top a loaf and a flower. There was always some play of chaffering at the door, barred, as in this drama, with a ribbon or scarf stretched between a distaff and a bident, the implements emblematic of woman and man. The exchange of a piece of money always closed the bargain and gained them entrance. Then, every woman, passing on in turn to the bridal pair, before lowering her basket, took from it a handful of grain and scattered it over each head, saying: "This is the bread God and our Lady send you. May you grow old together!"

The folk-ritual for burial and the improvisation of the laments by the wailers were so elaborate that the ecclesiastical authorities kept a jealous eye over their excesses. A decree of 1734 is peculiarly interesting on account of the

INTRODUCTION

recognition it supplies that these customs were bequests from a Pagan age. It declares that if the women who indulge in the abuse of mourning at funerals " continue to disturb the churchly office with lamentation and wailing and other such practices of paganism," the clergy shall cease all ministration and leave them with the body until they go home and " let the body alone, so that the service can be followed according to the usage of the Roman ritual."

Greater poetic interest belongs to the *laudi* in the Abruzzi dialect, examples of which are given in De Nino's fourth volume (*Usi e costumi abbruzzesi par* Antonio de Nino. 5 vols. Barbèra, Florence. 1879–1891). From the text of one of these, several verses are employed by D'Annunzio in the third Act. He greatly enhances their dramatic effect by putting them in the mouth of Candia, when with wandering, benumbed wits she repeats bits of the dialogue between the Sacred Mother and her suffering Son, half confusing her own sorrows over her son Aligi with those of the Mater Dolorosa.

In all such instances heightened beauty and significance are given to the Abruzzi usages with the surest and most delicate art. The throb of life animates it. Yet the homely truth to reality behind the adroit touches of art gifts the play with vigor and concreteness.

Even the passing reference of Splendore to the petticoat " of a dozen breadths' fulness " is true, for example, to the dress of the women of Scanno. The bridal raiment of green, also, " Of gold and silver the yoke is fashioned But all the rest like the quiet verdure," is true to the preference for green of the brides of Canzano.

Such games of rivalry for the straightest furrow, as that of which Candia reminds her son, were held at Sora. In presence of the old men the youths ran the plough from the crest of the hill to the foot of the valley, when the prize, a hat or a scarf, was adjudged.

The " barking " of the reapers " like dogs at each passer " was an ancient license of disorder at harvest time, called *fare l'incanata*. So, the call for the wine-jug was a custom belonging to the serenade of the bridal pair on the marriage night. The song over, the singers expected wine, cheese, and a loaf to be handed them outside the door.

As Aligi's cavern, the scene of the second Act, has its prototype in an actual cavern on

INTRODUCTION

the mountain in Abruzzia, from which Michetti
made sketches for stage use in the Milan production, so also the shepherd life, as it is presented especially in this Act, has its model in
reality. Their quiet existence, aloft among the
peaks, leaves the shepherds time to carve their
sheep-hooks, as Aligi did, and to achieve such
other artistry in wood as Aligi masters. Their
neighbor, the sky, makes dreamers of them, too,
like Aligi, and not infrequently poets. The
mountain affords them such comrades as Aligi
had in Malde, the treasure-diviner, the herb-
woman, wise in efficacious simples, and the
lofty, serene-minded Cosmo. Perhaps Cosmo
is not meant to differ greatly in nature from
the distinguished saint of the Morrone men-
tioned by Aligi, Pietro Celestino, who was made
Pope Célestin V. in 1294, but who, only a few
months afterwards, abjured the stateliness of
Rome for the hermit's retired life upon the
mountain-side. The habit of life, indicated by
Aligi, is that of the shepherds described by
Finamore (*Il pastore e la pastorizia in Abruzzo*
in *Archivo per lo studio della tradizioni popo-
lari,* IV. 190). They select a sheepstead in the
spring and collect their flocks, living near them
in caves or huts during the summer, but going

down to the village fortnightly for a three days'
rest; and in the autumn coming down with
their flocks, and going on with them either
toward Rome or Puglia. Through the valleys
and across the mountains they hear the singing
Pilgrims passing continually, as they so effec-
tively come and go in the stage directions of
the second Act, faring to and fro on the way
to such shrines as Splendore mentions in her
reassuring words to Mila, — Santa Maria
della Potenza, and the Incoronata.

On the eve of the Celebration of St. John's
Beheading (August 29) the Plaia or the Vir-
gine is climbed, according to custom, toward
midnight, so that the red disk of the August
sun may be seen at dawn from the hilltop.
To the beholder of the apparition of the saint's
bleeding head in the disk it was accounted, as
Aligi deemed it, a miraculous sign of God's
favor.

D'Annunzio himself maintains as to one of
the superstitions he has known how to weave
predominatingly into the plot, namely, the
sanctity of the fireplace as a refuge from violence, that it is Jewish rather than Italian. It
may be so. In any case he has exercised the
right of a poet to use for his higher verities

what he needs and has the art to employ vitally and well. It may be, too, that he has been peculiarly happy in grafting so distinctly Jewish a belief on the rest of his more peculiarly Christian and Latin beliefs, because there is an inner link of association between Mila's fireside and such a sanctuary from their pursuers as the Adonijahs and Joabs claimed when they "laid hold upon the horns of the altar." Feasts were held and burnt offerings were devoted to Jehovah on such altars. And similarly sacred to the gods of the hearthstone of the ancient race — the Lares and Penates — was the fireside of the Romans. The antique usage that marks the fireplace and sets it apart as the altar or temple of the homestead is architecturally preserved in ancient Italian buildings by the monumental setting of the hearthstone above the level of the floor and the prominent hood to the chimney. The utility of this arrangement, as usual with folk-myths, has not hindered, but rather attracted, a religious explanation.

Such a fireplace is an imporant trait of the stage directions in the first Act for the scene-setting of the home of the Di Roio family. It is in accord, like all the rest of the furnishings

INTRODUCTION

of the house, with the record De Nino supplies
of the typical Abruzzi homestead.

When the daughter of the alien, of the sorcerer Jorio, claims sanctuary at the hearth, she
claims it not alone because she is Christian and
therefore can justly make appeal to the God
of this hearth and this household. It is significant that she also makes her appeal by
virtue of the old laws of the hearthstone, to
gods of the Pagan race and the ancient kins-
folk. The sacredness of the fireplace as the
altar of each home is, in fact, not confined to
any race. The North American Indian, as
well as the Roman, regards it religiously. Such
faiths grow from a human root.

In the play, the hearth, like the Jewish
altar, becomes a mercy-seat, to be held inviolate from violence and also from profanation.
Mila seeks it as a shrine and shield from
violence. The kindred declare that she
profanes it.

The dependence of the second and third
Acts upon the Roman law of the absolute do-
minion of the father over the son, and the
extreme penalty for parricide of the sack and
the mastiff and the deep sea is justified by the
ancient Latin code, as given in the digest of

Modestinus (xlviii, tit. 9, § 9). The persistence
in the bucolic mind of such grim ancestral
morality causes such a code to outlive its
natural decay.

One of the allusions to the ancient credulities
of the Abruzzi which is most essential to the
plot is Aligi's vision in the first Act of Mila's
guardian angel standing behind her weeping,
and thus in silence revealing the innocency of
her wronged soul. The common faith in the
judgment of God upon the deeds of men being
made clear in a flash by the sudden sight of the
angel in tears finds expression in the proverbial
sayings: " If you would measure the offence,
look behind the right shoulder of him whom
you have offended." " If you make your sister
weep, you make the silent angel weep." " If
you forget to be just, the angel weeps."

Curious and interesting as all these veritable
traces of folk-lore may seem, they are but the
dry bones to which the poet has given flesh and
breath. Not alone the rich deep soil of primitive custom and religion in which he has rooted
the play, but the spirit of mystery primeval —
older than Christianity or any one religious influence — in which the play is wrapped, as in
the atmosphere necessary to its life, is indi-

cated by D'Annunzio himself in his " Triumph
of Death ":

" Rites of religions dead and forgotten sur-
vive there; incomprehensible symbols of poten-
cies long fallen into decay remain intact there;
habits of primitive peoples forever passed away
persist there, handed down without change
from generation to generation; rich customs,
foreign and useless, retained there are the wit-
nesses to the nobility and beauty of an anterior
life. . . . In all pomps and ceremonies, work
and play, in births and love, nuptials and funerals, — everywhere present and visible, there
is a georgic symbolism; everywhere the Titanic
generating Mother Earth is represented and
reverenced as the bosom whence sprang the
founts of all good and all happiness."

When Mila is left in the cave, in the second
Act, alone with the ecstasy and anguish of her
love for Aligi, and while she kneels before the
Christian symbol of motherhood, she turns also
to this hoary Earth, the mother of all motherhood, as the child in trouble to the all-embracing mother-heart.

The love which she and Aligi feel within
them is profoundly rooted in that elemental
mystery to which it has newly opened their

consciousness. It is more ancient far than any of the ties of habit and family to which Aligi has been the embodiment of faithful allegiance all his life before. Older than allegiance to the family or the clan is the allegiance of lover and beloved, as the individual man is prior to the tribal man.

As the play opens, the divine trouble of allegiance to this more fundamental power has come upon Aligi dimly. Forebodings of the woe of his attempted reconciliation of the two allegiances are sapping his energy. In the depths of his soul is divined the fatal approach of supreme love, the predestined child of this secret power of the older time. The shadow of this approach girds him about in slumber as in a shield by the side of the bride whose soul is no mate for his soul. It holds him aloof until Mila comes. Then it plunges his old allegiance, his most religiously dutiful subordination to the life of kindred and family, into vital conflict with the inward sense of the mystical power claiming a higher allegiance, a deeper, all-embracing reverence.

The situation is a dramatic bodying forth of further words of D'Annunzio upon the mystery brooding in the land of the antique blood:

INTRODUCTION

"Mystery intervenes in all events, envelops and constrains every existence; and supernatural life dominates, overwhelms, and absorbs ordinary life."

Put into action, this is the clash of the ordinary fealty with a fealty older, more personal, and through the art and the sacrifice begotten of love, more rewarding to spiritual life. The hand of the tribe has been ever against an overlordship of this spiritual kind, knitting together the clansman and the alien, and substituting for the child recruiting the solidarity of the clan, the Angel of Art recruiting the very soul of the clan. To burn as an Apostate Angel this Angel of Art along with the witch whose charm has awakened in the lover's soul the capacity to show it forth — this is the usual course of the clan. Only the Ornellas, the youngest and littlest of its generation, are as prompt to see and to save as its privileged heads, the Lazaros, are to desecrate and embrutalize.

Like Heinrich in Hauptmann's "Sunken Bell," Aligi is a dreamer. But unlike Heinrich, he is no waverer. His dream is true. To the divination it bestows he is true. As long as his soul and his senses are intact to repel

the benumbing influence of the potion he dis-
claims Mila's sacrifice.

All larger meanings involved in the action
are to be inferred as they are in life. Each
may behold for himself. Yet Ornella stands
behind the play, as the angel stood behind
Mila. For any, if any there be, who would
question the bearing of its conclusion, Ornella
is the rectification of any possible doubt or
misjudgment. Through the eyes of her vision
appears the transcendent loving of Mila.

No other works of D'Annunzio, not even
the beautiful " Francesca," reach such heights.
They have artistry, power, concrete truth to
life in common with " The Daughter of
Jorio "; but they do not approach it in that
inner truth to life which unveils the purity
and aspiration of the power of supreme love
in life and in art. That inner life of the power
of love hallows this tragedy. Hence the poet's
art gains an unerring potency of touch, and
it makes the loving of Mila worthy of a younger
brother of the Dante of the " Vita Nuova "
and the " Paradiso."

Inseparable from the power of this tragedy
to cause the deep things within to be heard —
" The deep things within that come from afar "

INTRODUCTION

— are the incomparably beautiful rhythms in which they are chanted.

They are the rhythms belonging to the land of the Abruzzi and to "many years ago." There, says the poet:

"Mystery and rhythm, these two essential elements of every cult, were everywhere scattered. Men and women constantly expressed their souls in song, accompanied by song all their labors under the roof or under the sky, celebrated by song life and death. Over cradles and winding-sheets undulated melodies slow and prolonged, very ancient, — as ancient, perhaps, as the race whose profound sadness they revealed. . . . Fixed in unalterable rhythm they seemed fragments of hymns belonging to immemorial liturgies, surviving the destruction of some great primordial mythus."

The poet seems to have loosed the pent-up sources of these immemorial rhythms. He has dared in part to invent a free dramatico-lyric verse, in part to recur to archaic forms of verse of like freedom. In this way he has clothed every motion and gesture, every quiver of the body of his drama, in a beauty begotten of "the antique blood."

Such music, sensitive to each catch of the

living breath of emotion, must seek a form more flexible than the iambic pentameters of English usage or the hexameters or Alexandrines of French. The beauty belonging to these in their perfection has yet led to a dull monotony of always-anticipated stress in the perpetuity of their dramatic use by modern dramatists. The artifice side of verse has been so over-emphasized, by limitation to a form shut out from the thrill of an unexpected cadence, that audiences instinctively flee the infliction of sitting out a modern poetic drama, despite the general superstition, because of its past glory, that it ought to be forever and only liked.

Since the only alternative offered by conventional usage is bald prose, even this has been gladly accepted in preference, and the penalty paid of a totally commonplace effect, usually as bare of the uplift and melody of art as a trolley car.

D'Annunzio has devised a better way. Heeding the secret of the manifold effects, — now of the ancient *laudi dramatiche* of his own Abruzzi, now of the austerely simple plain-song of the mediæval hymn, now of some strongly four-stressed Tuscan lyric of the twelfth century, or even the two-stressed line of the rustic charm, — he has varied his verse to suit every phase of emotion. He has used iambic ascending rhythms, in hendecasyllabic lines, generally, for the serener utterances, such as Candia's blessing in the espousal rites of Act I; strongly marked trochaic rhythms, in octosyllabic lines, for intense lyrical outpourings of spirit, such as Mila's song at the opening of Act II, and swiftly descending dactyllic rhythms, giving jets of voice to sharp seizures of feeling, such as the fierce outcry of the Chorus of the Kindred in Act III — *Tempia e tempia, i denti le sgrani* — " Temple to temple and shell out her teeth." Not only, moreover, by the frequent employment of a strong initial syllable, along with iambic or anapestic verse, and other such allowed liberties, but also by the intercalation of extra syllables or the omission of others within the normal foot, he has slowed or raced the pace of the line, in obedience to some push of thought or beat of purpose. So varied is the effect that the verse is as flexible as prose speech. Yet the impression is never lawless, for the verse never escapes the *ictus* of a pervading inward shapeliness. The artistic comeliness is felt along with the

INTRODUCTION

impetus each variation pours into the sway of the line.

Internal rhyme, assonance, and thrice repeated double rhymes still further prolong or break up the normal effects, so that to the fluency of the wave of speech is added some momentary shimmering of its surface, like the fleeting touches of the wind of the spirit otherwise viewless.

Such internal rhymes, repetitions, and assonances, for example, occur in the dialogue of Mila and Aligi in the second Act: *Pei monti coglierai le genzianellè Eper le spiagge le stelle marine.* — " To cull on the hilltop the blue gentian lonely, On the sea-shore only the star-fish flower." *Si cammina cammina lungo il mare.* — " I border the bordering stretches of sea-shore." Or such double rhymes appear as in Femo di Nerfa's: *Prima che la mano gli tàglino, Prima che nel sacco lo sèrrino, Col can mastino e lo gèttino, Al fiume in dove fa gorgo.* — " Before his right hand they shall sever, Before in the leathern sack they sew him With the savage mastiff and throw him Where the deep restless waters o'erflow him."

The tendency of English verse during the

INTRODUCTION

Elizabethan renaissance was toward a musical flexibility akin to D'Annunzio's. Shakespeare's verse, especially in his ripest work, showed the same tendency before it was regulated by Pope, who cut it into even lengths of ten syllables, with every even one stressed, as nearly as he could, by transposing, eliding, cutting off, or adding — a regulation still masking as well as marring the native woodnotes wild in all our modernized texts.

A similar flexibility belonged to Coleridge's " Christabel," wherein he recurred to the elder fashion of marking the rhythm sufficiently by stress to carry the voice as he willed it to go, instead of the dominant fashion of meting it into uniformly even lengths of counted syllables.

Each way should have its own uses for the modern poet according to the impressional effect he desires. The elder fashion is no more lawless than the one which has come to be so exclusively followed through the dominance of French influences at the English Court, in the seventeenth and eighteenth centuries, influences suiting the growing formalism of the English temperament. Indeed the elder fashion requires a more expert metrical handling, while the other is more open to mediocre poetic ability.

It would be well for the closer hold of poetic art on life, especially for dramatic use, if less automatically regulated verse should be revived and developed in England, above all in America, — such flexible verse as D'Annunzio has revived and developed in " The Daughter of Jorio."

To translate such verse into set metres of blank verse or Alexandrines, in no way corresponding to its peculiar variability, would be like prisoning a live creature. To do it violence by uniformly substituting strong endings for weak endings; to reiterate uniformly the metre arbitrarily chosen to begin with; to exclude all grace of internal rhyme would be like binding a mobile thing from any fluttering. Surely it would be to cage the bird whose sensitive wings the genius of D'Annunzio has freed.

It has fallen to my especial share in this joint translation to give to it a verse form. It has seemed to me hopeless, — and my colleagues are agreed with me in this view — to attempt to give any glimmering impression of the rhythmic beauty essential to the mystical

INTRODUCTION

soul of this tragedy, save by seeking to re-
produce for English ears, by similarly free
methods in freely stressed English verse, an
audible impression corresponding to the impression which the stresses of the Italian verse
have made on my ear as they were spoken.
Hence the desire has been not to be led by
the eye, nor to transliterate analytically the
Italian effects in some recognized forms of
imitative prosody, but merely to listen and
echo in English some faint synthetic reflex of
the flowing music.

CHARLOTTE PORTER.

ILLUSTRATIONS

DRAMATIS PERSONÆ

Lazaro Di Roio, *Father of Aligi*

Candia Della Leonessa, *Mother of Aligi*

Aligi, *The Shepherd-Artist*

Splendore, Favetta, Ornella, *Aligi's Sisters*

Vienda Di Giave, *Aligi's Bride*

Maria Di Giave, *Mother of the Bride*

Teodula Di Cinzio, La Cinerella, Monica Della Cogna, Anna Di Bova, Felavia, La Catalana, Maria Cora : *The Kindred*

Mila Di Codra, *the Daughter of Jorio the Sorcerer dalle Farne*

Femo Di Nerfa

Jenne Dell' Eta

Iona Di Midia

The Old Herbwoman

The Saint of the Mountain

The Treasure Diviner

The Devil-Possessed Youth

A Shepherd

Another Shepherd

A Reaper

Another Reaper

DRAMATIS PERSONÆ

THE CROWD OF PEOPLE
THE CHORUS OF THE KINDRED
THE CHORUS OF REAPERS
THE CHORUS OF WAILERS

SCENE: The Land of the Abruzzi

TIME: Many years ago.   (Placed about the sixteenth century by the Painter Michetti, who designed the scenes and costumes for the initial production in Milan).

THE
DAUGHTER OF JORIO

Act I. — Scene I.

A ROOM *on the ground floor of a rustic house. The large entrance door opens on a large sunlit yard. Across the door is stretched, to prevent entrance, a scarlet woollen scarf, held in place at each end by a forked hoe and a distaff. At one side of the door jamb is a waxen cross to keep off evil spirits. A smaller closed door, with its architrave adorned with boxwood green, is on the wall at the right, and close against the same wall are three ancient wooden chests. At the left, and set in the depth of the wall, is a chimney and fire-place with a prominent hood; and a little at one side a small door, and near this an ancient loom. In the room are to be*

1

seen such utensils and articles of furniture as
tables, benches, hasps, a swift, and hanks of flax
and wool hanging from light ropes drawn between nails or hooks.   Also to be seen are jugs,
dishes, plates, bottles and flasks of various sizes
and materials, with many gourds, dried and
emptied.   Also an ancient bread and flour chest,
the cover of it having a carved panel represent-
ing the image of the Madonna.   Beside this
the water basin and a rude old table.   Sus-
pended from the ceiling by ropes is a wide,
broad board laden with cheeses.   Two windows,
iron-grated and high up from the ground, give
light, one at each side of the large door, and
in each of the gratings is stuck a bunch of red
buckwheat to ward off evil.

SPLENDORE, FAVETTA, ORNELLA, the three
young sisters, are kneeling each in front of
one of the three chests containing the wedding
dresses.   They are bending over them and picking out suitable dresses and ornaments for the
bride.   Their gay, fresh tones are like the
chanting of morning songs.

2

SPLENDORE

What's your will, our own Vienda?

FAVETTA

What's your will, our dear new sister?

SPLENDORE

Will you choose the gown of woolen,
Would you sooner have the silken,
Sprayed with flowrets red and yellow?

ORNELLA [*singing*]

Only of green shall be my arraying.
Only of green for Santo Giovanni,
For mid the green meadows he came to seek
    me,
Oili, Oili, Oila!

SPLENDORE

Look! Here is the bodice of wondrous em-
    broidery,
And the yoke with the gleaming thread of
    silver,

3

Petticoat rich of a dozen breadths' fulness,
Necklace strung with hundred-beaded coral, —
All these given you by your new mother.

ORNELLA [*singing*]

Only of green be or gown or bridal chamber!
Oili, oili, oila!

FAVETTA

What 's your will, our own Vienda?

SPLENDORE

What 's your will, our dear new sister?

ORNELLA

Pendant earrings, clinging necklace,
Blushing ribbons, cherry red?
Hear the ringing bells of noonday,
Hear the bells ring out high noon!

SPLENDORE

See the kindred hither coming,
On their heads the hampers bearing,

4

Hampers laden with wheat all golden,
And you yet not dressed and ready!

ORNELLA

Bounding, rebounding,
Sheep pass, the hills rounding.
The wolf, through valleys winding,
The nut he seeks is finding, —
The pistachio nut is finding.
See, the Bride of the Morning!
Matinal as the field-mouse
Going forth at the dawning,
As the woodchuck and squirrel.
Hear, O hear, the bells' whirl!

[*All these words are spoken very swiftly,
and at the close* ORNELLA *laughs joyously, her
two sisters joining with her.*]

THE THREE SISTERS

Oh! Aligi, why then don't you come?

SPLENDORE

Oh! in velvet then must you dress?

5

FAVETTA

Seven centuries quite, must you rest
With your beautiful, magical Spouse?

SPLENDORE

O your father stays at the harvesting,
Brother mine, and the star of the dawning
In his sickle-blade is showing, —
In his sickle, no rest knowing.

FAVETTA

And your mother has flavored the wine-cup
And anise-seed mixed with the water,
Sticking cloves in the roast meat
And sweet thyme in the cheeses.

SPLENDORE

And a lamb of the flock we have slaughtered,
Yea, a yearling, but fattened one season,
With head markings and spottings of sable,
For the Bride and the Bridegroom.

OF JORIO

FAVETTA

And the mantle, long-sleeved, and cowl-
  hooded,
For Astorgio we chose it and kept it, —
For the long-lived gray man of the mountain,
So our fate upon that he foretell us.

ORNELLA

And to-morrow will be San Giovanni,
Dear, my brother! with dawn, San Giovanni!
Up the Plaia hill then shall I hie me,
To behold once again the head severed —
In the sun's disc, the holy head severed,
On the platter all gleaming and golden,
Where again the blood runs, flows and babbles.

FAVETTA

Up, Vienda! head all golden,
Keeping long vigil; O golden sweet tresses!
Now they harvest in the grain-fields
Wheat as golden as your tresses.

7

SPLENDORE

Our mother was saying: " Now heed me!
Three olives I nurtured here with me;
Unto these now a plum have I added.
Ay! three daughters, and, also, a daughter."

ORNELLA

Come, Vienda, golden-plum girl!
Why delay you? Are you writing
To the sun a fair blue letter
That to-night it know no setting?

[*She laughs and the other sisters join in
with her. From the small door enters their
mother,* CANDIA DELLA LEONESSA.]

CANDIA [*playfully chiding*]

Ah! you magpies, sweet cicales!
Once for over-joy of singing
One was burst upon the poplar.
Now the cock 's no longer crowing
To awaken tardy sleepers.
Only sing on these cicales, —

8

These cicales of high noonday.
These three magpies take my roof-tree —
Take my door's wood for a tree-branch.
Still the new child does not heed them.
Oh! Aligi, Aligi, dear fellow!

[*The door opens. The beardless bridegroom appears. He greets them with a grave
voice, fixed eyes, and in an almost religious
manner.*]

ALIGI

All praise to Jesus and to Mary!
You, too, my mother, who this mortal
Christian flesh to me have given,
Be you blessèd, my dear mother!
Blessèd be ye, also, sisters,
Blossoms of my blood!
For you, for me, I cross my forehead,
That never there come before us to thwart us
The enemy subtle, in death, in life,
In heat of sun, or flame of fire,
Or poison, or any enchantment,

9

Or sweat unholy the forehead moist'ning.
Father, and Saviour, and Holy Spirit!

[*The sisters cross themselves and go out
by the small door, carrying the bridal dresses.
*ALIGI *approaches his mother as if in a dream.*]

CANDIA

Flesh of my flesh, thus touch I your forehead
With bread, with this fair wheaten loaf of
    white flour,
Prepared in this bowl of a hundred years old,
Born long before thee, born long before me,
Kneaded long on the board of a hundred years
    old
By these hands that have tended and held you.
On the brow, thus, I touch: Be it sunny and
    clear!
I touch thus the breast: Be it free from all
    sighing!
I touch this shoulder, and that: Be it strong!
Let them bear up your arms for long labor!
Let her rest there her head gray or golden!
And may Christ to you speak and you heed him!

10

[*With the loaf she makes the sign of the cross above her son, who has fallen on his knees before her.*]

ALIGI

I lay down and meseemed of Jesus I dreamed.
He came to me saying: " Be not fearful."
San Giovanni said to me: " Rest in safety.
Without holy candles thou shalt not die."
Said he: " Thou shalt not die the death ac-
    cursèd."
And you, you have cast my lot in life, mother,
Allotted the bride you have chosen for me, —
Your son, and here, within your own house,
    mother,
You have brought her to couple with me,
That she slumber with me on my pillow,
That she eat with me out of my platter.
Then I was pasturing flocks on the mountain.
Now back to the mountain I must be turning.

[*His mother touches his head with the palm of her hand as if to chase away evil thoughts.*]

CANDIA

Rise up, my son! You are strangely talking.
All your words are now changing in color,
As the olive tree changes pressed by the
  breezes.

[*He rises, as if in a daze.*]

ALIGI

But where is my father? Still nowhere I see
  him.

CANDIA

Gone to the harvesting, out with the reapers,
The good grain reaping, by grace of our
  Saviour.

ALIGI

I reaped once, too, by his body shaded,
Ere I was signed with the cross on my
  forehead,
When my brow scarcely reached up to his
  haunches.
But on my first day a vein here I severed, —
Here where the scar stays. Then with leaves
  he was bruising

12

The while he stanched the red blood from
     flowing,
" Son Aligi," said he unto me, " Son Aligi,
Give up the sickle and take up the sheep-
     crook:
Be you a shepherd and go to the moun-
     tain."
This his command was kept in obedience.

CANDIA

Son of mine, what is this pain the heart of
     you hurting?
What dream like an incubus over you hovers,
That these your words are like a wayfarer,
Sitting down on his road at night's coming,
Who is halting his footsteps for knowing,
Beyond attaining is his heart's desiring,
Past his ears' hearing the Ave Maria.

ALIGI

Now to the mountain must I be returning.
Mother, where is my stout shepherd's sheep-
     hook

13

Used to the pasture paths, daily or nightly?
Let me have that, so the kindred arriving,
May see thereupon all the carving I 've carved.

[*His mother takes the shepherd's crook
from the corner of the fireplace.*]

CANDIA

Lo! here it is, son of mine, take it: your sisters
Have hung it with garlands for Santo Giovanni,
With pinks red and fragrant festooned it.

ALIGI [*pointing out the carving on it*]

And I have them here on the bloodwood all
  with me,
As if by the hand I were leading my sisters.
So, along they go with me threading green
  pathways,
Guarding them, mother, — these three virgin
  damsels, —
See! three bright angels here over them hover,
And three starry comets, and three meek doves
  also.

14

And a flower for each one I have carved here,

The growing half-moon and the sun I have
carved here;

This is the priestly stole; and this is the cup
sacramental;

And this is the belfry of San Biagio.

And this is the river, and this my own cabin;

[*with mystery, as if with second sight*]

But who, who is this one who stands in my
doorway?

CANDIA

Aligi, why is it you set me to weeping!

ALIGI

And see at the end here that in the ground
enters,

Here are the sheep, and here also their shepherd,

And here is the mountain where I must be
going,

Though you weep, though I weep, my mother!

15

[*He leans on the crook with both hands, resting his head upon them, lost in his thoughts.*]

CANDIA

But where then is Hope?   What have you
made of her, son?

ALIGI

Her face has shone on me seldom;
Carve her, I could not, sooth!   mother.

[*From a distance a savage clamor rises.*]

Mother, who shouts out so loud there?

CANDIA

The harvesters heated and frenzied,
From the craze of their passions defend them,
From sins of their blood San Giovanni restrain
them!

ALIGI

Ah! Who then has drawn but that scarf there,
Athwart the wide door of our dwelling,

16

Leaning on it the forked hoe and distaff,
That naught enter in that is evil?
Ah! Lay there the ploughshare, the wain,
　　and the oxen,
Pile stones there against both the door-posts,
With slaked lime from all of the lime-kilns,
The bowlder with footprints of Samson,
And Maella Hill with its snow-drifts!

CANDIA

What is coming to birth in your heart, son
　　of mine?
Did not Christ say to you, " Be not fear-
　　ful "?
Are you awake? Heed the waxen cross there,
That was blessed on the Day of Ascension,
The door-hinges, too, with holy water
　　sprinkled,
No evil spirit can enter our doorway,
Your sisters have drawn the scarlet scarf 'cross
　　it, —
The scarlet scarf you won in the field-match
Long before you ever became a shepherd,

17

In the match that you ran for the straightest
 furrow, —
(You still remember it, son of mine?)   Thus
 have they stretched it
So that the kindred who must pass through
 there
Offer what gifts they choose when they enter.
Why do you ask, for you well know our
 custom?

ALIGI

Mother! mother! I have slept years seven
 hundred —
Years seven hundred! I come from afar off.
I remember no longer the days of my cradle.

CANDIA

What ails you, son?   Like one in a dazement
 you answer.
Black wine was it your bride poured out for
 you?
And perhaps you drank it while yet you were
 fasting,

18

So that your mind is far off on a journey?
O Mary, blest Virgin! do thou grant me
    blessing!

The voice of Ornella *singing the nuptial
song.*

Only of green shall be my arraying,
Only of green for Santo Giovanni.
Oili, oili, oila!

[*The* Bride *appears dressed in green and
is brought forward joyously by the sisters.*]

SPLENDORE

Lo! the bride comes whom we have apparelled
With all the joy of the spring-time season.

FAVETTA

Of gold and silver the yoke is fashioned,
But all the rest like the quiet verdure.

ORNELLA

You, mother, take her! in your arms take her!
O dear my mother, take and console her!

19

SPLENDORE

Shedding tears at the bedside we found
    her,
Thus lamenting for thinking so sorely
Of the gray head at home left so lonely.

ORNELLA

Of the jar full of pinks in the window
Her dear face not again shall lean over.
You, mother, take her! in your arms take her!

CANDIA

Daughter, daughter, with this loaf in blessing
I have touched my own son. Lo! now I di-
    vide it,
And over your fair shining head I now break
    it.
May our house have increase of abundance!
Be thou unto the dough as good leaven
That may swell it out over the bread-board!
Bring unto me peace and ah! do not bring
    strife to me!

20

THE THREE SISTERS

So be it! We kiss the earth, mother!

[*They kiss the ground by leaning over and touching it with forefinger and middle finger, and then touching their lips.* ALIGI *is kneeling on one side as if in deep prayer.*]

CANDIA

O now daughter mine to my house be
As the spindle is unto the distaff;
As unto the skein is the spindle;
And as unto the loom is the shuttle!

THE THREE SISTERS

So be it! We kiss the earth, mother!

CANDIA

O Vienda! new daughter, child blessèd!
Lo! midst home and pure food thus I place
   you.
Lo! The walls of this house — the four corners!

21

God willing, the sun rises there; sinks there,
  God willing!
This is the northward, this is the southward.
The ridgepole this, the eaves with nests
  hanging,
And the chain and the crane with the and-
  irons;
There the mortar the white salt is crushed in,
And there, too, the crock it is kept in.
O new daughter! I call you to witness
How midst home things and pure food I
  place you
Both for this life and life everlasting.

THE THREE SISTERS

So be it! We kiss the earth, mother!

[VIENDA *rests her head, weeping, on the
shoulder of the mother.* CANDIA *embraces her,
still holding a half-loaf in each hand. The cry
of the reapers is heard nearer.* ALIGI *rises like
one suddenly wakened and goes toward the
door. The sisters follow him.*]

FAVETTA

Now by the great heat are the reapers all
 maddened,
They are barking and snapping like dogs at
 each passer.

SPLENDORE

Now the last of the rows they are reaching,
With the red wine they never mix water.

ORNELLA

At the end of each row, they are drinking,
In the shade of the stack the jug lying.

FAVETTA

Lord of heaven! The heat is infernal,
At her tail bites the old gammer serpent.

ORNELLA [*chanting*]

Oh, for mercy! Wheat and wheat, and stubble, stubble,
First in sun burn the sickles, then wounds they
 trouble.

SPLENDORE

Oh mercy for father! for his arms tired,
And all his veins with labor swollen.

ORNELLA

O Aligi! you saddest of grooms
Keeping yet in your nostrils sleep's fumes!

FAVETTA

O, you know very well the rhyme turned about.
You have placed the good loaf in the jug,
You have poured the red wine in the sack.

SPLENDORE

Lo! now the kindred! Lo! now the women!
    they are coming.
Up, up! Vienda! and cease your weeping.
Mother! How now! They are coming. Set
    her free then.
Up! Golden tresses, cease your weeping!
You have wept too long. Your fine eyes are
    reddened!

24

[VIENDA *dries her tears on her apron and taking the apron up by the two corners receives in it the two pieces of the loaf from the mother.*]

CANDIA

In blood and in milk return it to me!
Goldenhair, come now, sit on the settle.
Oh! Aligi, you too, come sit here! and wake up!
One of you here, one of you there, thus stay ye,
Children, thus, at each side of the door.
Be it wide open for all to see in there
The wide bed so wide that in order to fill it —
The mattress to fill — I used up the straw-
    stack.
Ay! the whole of the stack to the bare pole,
With the crock sticking up on the tiptop!

[CANDIA *and* SPLENDORE *place a small bench each side of the door, where the couple sit composed and silent, looking at each other.* ORNELLA *and* FAVETTA *looking out toward the road at the large door. The yard is in dazzling sunlight.*]

25

FAVETTA

See! They are coming up the road slowly
In single file, all: Teodula di Cinzio
And Cinerella, Monica, Felavia,
And Catalana delle Tre Bisacce,
Anna di Bova, Maria Cora . . . but who is
    the last one?

CANDIA

Come on then, Splendore, do help me spread
    out now
The bedspread I wove of silk doubled,
Woven for you, Vienda, dear green bud,
As green as the grass of the meadow,
The sweet grass, early bee, where you hover.

ORNELLA

Who is last? Can you tell us, Vienda?
Oh! I see yellow grain in the hampers,
And it glitters like gold. Who can she be?
Gray at the temple, beneath the white linen,
Gray as the feathery bryony branches.

26

FAVETTA

Your mommy! dear child, is she your mommy?

[VIENDA *rises suddenly as if to rush to her mother. In so doing she lets the bread fall from her apron. She stops, shocked.* ALIGI *rises and stands so as to prevent the mother from seeing.*]

ORNELLA [*greatly concerned, in a frightened voice*]

O Lord save us! Pick it up again.
Pick it up, kiss it, ere mamma see it.

[VIENDA, *terrified and overwhelmed by frightful superstition, is stricken immovable, rigid, staring at the two half-loaves with glassy eyes.*]

FAVETTA

Pick it up, kiss it, sad is the angel.
Make a vow silently, promise greatly,
Call on San Sisto, lest Death should appear.

[*From within are heard the blows given with the hand on mattress and pillows and the wind carries to the ear the clamor of the reapers.*]

ORNELLA

San Sisto! San Sisto!
Oh! hear ye, and list, oh!
Black death, evil sprite,
By day, by night,
Chase from our walls!
Drive from our souls!
Oh! crumble and tear
The evil eye's snare,
As the sign of the cross I make!

[*While murmuring the conjuring words she rapidly gathers up the two half-loaves, pressing each to* VIENDA'*s lips, kissing them herself, and then placing each in the apron, making the sign of the cross over them. She then leads the bridal couple to their benches, as the first of the women kindred appears at the door with the offerings, stopping in front of the scarlet scarf. The women each carry on the head a hamper of wheat adorned with flowing*

28

*ribbons of various colors. On each basket rests
a loaf of bread, and on top of each loaf a wild
flower.* Ornella *and* Favetta *take each one
end of the scarf while still leaving hoe and
distaff in place against the wall, but so posed
as to bar entrance.*]

FIRST WOMAN, TEODULA DI CINZIO

Ohé! Who watches the bridges?

FAVETTA and ORNELLA [*in unison*]

Love open-eyed and Love blind.

TEODULA

To cross over there I desire.

FAVETTA

To desire is not to acquire.

TEODULA

I clambered the mountain ridges,
Now down through the valley I 'll wind.

29

ORNELLA

The torrent has taken the bridges,
Too swift runs the river, you 'll find.

TEODULA

Set me over in your boat.

FAVETTA

She leaks too fast to keep afloat.

TEODULA

I 'll calk her with tow and resin.

ORNELLA

Leaks full seven split and stove her.

TEODULA

Then I 'll give you pieces seven.
On your shoulder bear me over.

FAVETTA

Oh, no! Help of mine you must lack.
The wild water fills me with fright.

30

THE FEAST OF ESPOUSAL.

Act I., Page 31.

TEODULA

Lend me a lift on your back.
I 'll give you this silver piece bright.

ORNELLA

Too little!   Your eight bits, indeed,
Would not keep my ribbons new.

TEODULA

Tuck up your skirt.   Plunge in bare-kneed.
A ducat of gold I 'll give to you.

[*The first woman,* TEODULA, *gives* OR-
NELLA *a piece of money   She receives it in her
left hand, while the other women come closer
to the door.   The bridal pair remain seated and
silent.* CANDIA *and* SPLENDORE *enter from the
small door.*]

ORNELLA and FAVETTA [*in unison*]

Pass on then, O you fair Lady!
And all these in your company!

31

[ORNELLA *puts the money in her bosom
and takes away the distaff,* FAVETTA, *the hoe.
They then leave both leaning against the wall.*
ORNELLA, *with a quick movement, withdraws
the scarf, making it wave like a slender pen-
nant. The women then enter one by one, in
line, still holding their baskets balanced on
their heads.*]

TEODULA

Peace be with you, Candia della Leonessa!
And peace, too, with you, son of Lazaro di
    Roio!
And peace to the bride whom Christ has given!

[*She places her basket at the bride's feet
and, taking out of it a handful of wheat, she
scatters it over* VIENDA'*s head. She then takes
another handful and scatters it over* ALIGI'*s.*]

This is the peace that is sent you from Heaven:
That on the same pillow your hair may whiten,
On the same pillow to old age ending.
Nor sin nor vengeance be between you,

Falsehood nor wrath, but love, love only,
Daily, till time for the long, long journey.

[*The next woman repeats the same cere-
mony and action, the others meanwhile remain-
ing in line awaiting their turn, with the hampers
on their heads. The last one, the mother of the
bride, remains motionless near the threshold,
and dries her face of tears and perspiration.
The noise of the riotous reapers increases and
seems to come nearer. Besides this noise, from
time to time, in pauses, now and again the ringing of bells is heard.*]

CINERELLA

For this is peace and this is plenty.

[*Suddenly a woman's cry is heard outside,
coming from the yard.*]

THE VOICE OF THE UNKNOWN WOMAN

Help! Help! For Jesus' sake, our Saviour!
People of God, O people of God, save ye me!

[*Running, panting from fright and exer-
tion, covered with dust and briars, like a hart
run down by a pack of hunting dogs, a woman
enters. Her face is covered by a mantle. She
looks about bewildered, and withdraws to the
corner near the fireplace, opposite to the bridal
pair.*]

THE UNKNOWN WOMAN

People of God! O save ye me!
The door there! O shut tight the door there,
Put ye up all the bars! Securely. —
They are many, and all have their sickles.
They are crazed, — crazed with heat and
    strong drinking.
They are brutal with lust and with cursing.
Me would they hunt, — they would seize me;
They would hunt me, they would seize me, —
    me, —
The creature of Christ, ay, me, —
The unhappy one, doing no evil!
Passing I was — alone — by the roadside. —
They saw me. — They cried. — They insulted.

They hurled sods and stones. — They chased
    me. —
Ay! like unto hounds that are hungry,
They would seize me and tear me and torture.
They are following me, O most wretched!
They are hunting me down, people of God!
Help ye! Save me! The door, O shut it to!
The door! — They are maddened — will enter!
They will take me from here, — from your
    hearthstone —
(The deed even God cannot pardon) ! —
From your hearthstone that blest is and sacred
(And aught else but that deed God par-
    dons) —
And my soul is baptized, — I am Christian —
Oh! help! O for San Giovanni's sake, help
    me!
For Mary's sake, her of the seven dolors!
For the sake of my soul. — For your own
    soul!

[*She stays by the hearth, all the women
gathering at the side opposite her.* VIENDA
close to her mother and godmother. ALIGI

*stands outside the circle unmoved, leaning on
his crook. Suddenly* ORNELLA *rushes to the
door, closes it, and bars it. A somewhat in-
imical murmur arises from the circle of
women.*]

Ah! tell me your name, — how they call
    you, —
Your name, that wherever I wander,
Over mountains, in valleys I bless it,
You, who in pity are first here,
Though in years yours are least in the count-
    ing!

[*Overcome she lets herself drop on the
hearth, bowed over upon herself with her head
resting on her knees. The women are huddled
together like frightened sheep.* ORNELLA
steps forward toward the stranger.]

ANNA

Who is this woman? Holy Virgin!

MARIA

And is this the right way to enter
The dwelling of God-fearing people?

36

MONICA

And Candia, you! What say you?

LA CINERELLA

Will you let the door stay bolted?

ANNA

Is the last to be born of your daughters,
The first to command in your household?

LA CATALANA

She will bring down upon you bad fortune,
The wandering she-dog, for certain!

FELAVIA

Did you mark how she entered that instant
While yet Cinerella was pouring
On Vienda her handful of wheat flour
Ere Aligi had got his share fully?

[ORNELLA *goes a step nearer the wretched
fugitive.* FAVETTA *leaves the circle and joins
her.*]

37

MONICA

How now!   Are we, then, to remain here,
With our baskets still on our heads loaded?

MARIA

Sure it would be a terrible omen
To put down on the ground here our baskets
Before giving our offerings to them.

MARIA DI GIAVE

My daughter, may Saint Luke defend you!
Saint Mark and Saint Matthew attend you!
Grope for your scapulary round your neck
    hanging,
Hold it closely and offer your prayer.

[Splendore, *too, comes forward and joins
the sisters. The three girls stand before the
fugitive, who is still prostrate, panting and
trembling with fear.*]

ORNELLA

You are over sore-pressed, sister,

And dusty and tired, you tremble.
Weep no more, since now you are safe here.
You are thirsty. Your drink is your tears.
Will you drink of our water and wine? Your
    face bathe?

[*She takes a small bowl, draws water from
the earthen receptacle and pours wine into it.*]

FAVETTA

Are you of the valleys or elsewhere?
Do you come from afar? And whither
Do you now bend your steps, O woman!
All desolate thus by the roadside!

SPLENDORE

Some malady ails you, unlucky one?
A vow then of penitence made you?
To the Incoronata were travelling?
May the Virgin answer your prayers!

[*The fugitive lifts her head slowly and cau-
tiously, with her face still hidden in the
mantle.*]

39

ORNELLA [*offering the bowl*]

Will you drink, now, daughter of Jesus?

[*From outside a noise is heard as of bare
feet shuffling in the yard and voices murmuring. The stranger, again stricken with fear,
does not drink from the proffered bowl but
places it on the hearth and retires trembling to
the further corner of the chimney.*]

THE UNKNOWN ONE

They are here, oh, they come! They are
    seeking
For me! They will seize me and take me.
For mercy's sake, answer not, speak not.
They will go if they think the house empty,
And do nothing evil; but if you
Are heard, if you speak or you answer
They will certainly know I have entered.
They will open the door, force it open.
With the heat and the wine they are frenzied,
Mad dogs! and here is but one man,
And many are they and all have their sickles,

Their scythes. — Oh! for dear pity's sake,
For the sake of these innocent maidens,
For your sake, dear daughter of kindness!
　You, women holy!

THE BAND OF REAPERS [*in chorus outside at the door*]

The dwelling of Lazaro! Surely
Into this house entered the woman.
— They have closed the door, they have barred
　it!
— Look out for her there in the stubble.
— Search well in the hay there, Gonzelvo.
— Hah! Hah! In the dwelling of Lazaro,
Right into the maw of the wolf. Hah! Hah!
— O! Candia della Leonessa!
Ho! all of you there! Are you dead?
　　　　　　　　[*They knock at the door.*]
Oh! Candia della Leonessa!
Do you offer a shelter to harlots?
— Do you find that you need such temptation
To still the fain flesh of your husband?
— If the woman be there, I say, open!
Open the door, good folks, give her to us

41

And on a soft bed we will lay her.
— Bring her out to us! Bring her out to us,
For we only want to know her better.
To the hay-cock, the hay-cock, the hay-cock!

[*They knock and clamor.* ALIGI *moves toward the door.*]

THE UNKNOWN ONE [*whispering imploringly*]

Young man, O young man, pray have mercy!
O have mercy! Do not open!
Not for my sake, not mine, but for others,
Since they will not seize now on me only,
Since imbruted are they. You must hear it! —
In their voices? — How now the fiend holds
    them?
The bestial mad fiend of high noonday,
The sweltering dog-days' infection.
If they gain entry here, what can you do?

[*The greatest excitement prevails among the women, but they restrain themselves.*]

LA CATALANA

Ye see now to what shame we all are submitted,

We women of peace here, for this woman,
She who dares not show her face to us!

ANNA

Open, Aligi, open the door there,
But wide enough to let her pass out.
Grip hold of her and toss her out there,
Then close and bar the entrance, giving praises
To Lord Jesus our salvation.
And perdition overtake all wretches!

[*The shepherd turns toward the woman,
hesitating.* ORNELLA, *stepping forward, stops
his way; making a sign of silence, she goes
to the door.*]

ORNELLA

Who is there? Who knocks at the door there?

VOICES OF THE REAPERS [*outside, all confusedly*]

— Silence there! Hush up! Hush—sh!
Hush—sh!
—— There is some one within who is speaking,
— O Candia della Leonessa,

Is it you who are speaking? Open! Open!
— We are the reapers here of Norca,
All the company are we of Cataldo.

ORNELLA

I am not Candia. For Candia is busied now.
Abroad is she since early morning.

A VOICE

And you? Say who are you then?

ORNELLA

I belong to Lazaro, Ornella,
My father is Lazaro di Roio.
But ye, say ye, why ye have come here?

A VOICE

Open, we but want to look inside there.

ORNELLA

Open, that I cannot. For my mother
Locked me in here with her kindred
Going out, for we are marrying.

44

The betrothal we are having of my brother,
Aligi, the shepherd, who is taking
To wife here, Vienda di Giave.

A VOICE

Did you then not let in a woman,
But a short while ago, a woman frightened?

ORNELLA

A woman?   Then in peace go away.
Seek ye elsewhere to find her.
O reapers of Norca!   I return to my loom here,
For each cast that is lost by my shuttle
Will be lost and can never be gathered.
God be with you to keep you from evil,
O ye reapers of Norca!   May he give you
Strength for your work in the grain fields
Till by evening you reach the end of your labor,
And I, also, poor woman, the ending
Of the breadth of this cloth I am weaving.

[*Suddenly at the side window two muscular
hands seize the iron bars and a brutal face peers
in.*]

45

THE REAPER [*shouting in a loud voice*]

Ho! Captain! the woman is in there!
She's inside! She's inside! The youngster
Was fooling us here, yes, the youngster!
The woman is in there! See, inside there,
In the corner. I see her, I see her!
And there too is the bride and the bridegroom,
And the kindred who brought them their
 presents.
This is the feast of the grain-pouring spousal.
Ah, ho! Captain! A fine lot of girls there!

CHORUS OF REAPERS [*outside*]

— If the woman's within, we say, open!
For you it is shame to protect her.
— Send her out here! Send her out here!
And we will give her some honey.
— Ho! open there, open, you, and give her
 to us.
— To the hay-cock with her, to the hay-cock.

 [*They clamor and shout. The women inside are all confused and agitated. The un-*

*known one keeps in the shadow, shrinking close
to the wall, as if she sought to sink herself
in it.*]

CHORUS OF KINDRED

— O help us, O holy Virgin!
Is this what the vigil gives us,
The eve of Santo Giovanni?
— What disgrace is this you give us, — what
    sorrow
This that you give us, Beheaded one! —
Just to-day of all days.
— Candia, have you lost your reason?
— O Candia, have you lost your senses?
— Ornella, and all your sisters with you?
— She was always a bit of a madcap.
— Give her up to them, give her, give her
To these hungry, ravening wolves!

THE REAPER [*still holding the bars*]

Shepherd Aligi, Oho! shepherd Aligi,
Will you give, at your feast of espousal,
A place to a sheep that is rotten, —

A sheep that is mangy and lousy?
Take care she infect not your sheepfold,
Or give to your wife her contagion.
O Candia della Leonessa,
Know you whom in your home there you
    harbor,
In your home there with your new-found
    daughter?
The daughter of Jorio, the daughter
Of the Sorcerer of Codra!
She-dog roamer o'er mountains and valleys,
A haunter of stables and straw-stacks,
Mila the shameless?   Mila di Codra.
The woman of stables and straw-heaps,
Very well known of all companies;
And now it has come to be our turn, —
The turn of the reapers of Norca.
Send her out here, send her out here!
We must have her, have her, have her!

[ALIGI, *pale and trembling, advances toward
the wretched woman, who remains persistently
in the shadow; and pulling off her mantle, he
uncovers her face.*]

48

MILA DI CODRA

No! No! It is not true! A cruel lie!
A cruel lie! Do not believe him,
Do not believe what such a dog says!
It is but the cursèd wine speaking
And out of his mouth bubbling evil.
If God heard it, may He to poison
Turn his black words, and he drown in 't!
No! It is not true. A cruel lie!

[*The three sisters stop their ears while the
reaper renews his vituperations.*]

THE REAPER

You shameless one! you are common,
Well known are you as the ditches,
The field-grass to dry straw turning,
Under your body's sins burning,
Men for your body have gambled
And fought with pitchforks and sickles.
Only wait just a bit for your man, Candia,
And you 'll see! He 'll come back to you
    bandaged,

49

For sure! From a fight with Rainero,
A fight in the grain-field of Mispa, —
For whom but for Jorio's daughter?
And now you keep her in your home, here,
To give her to your man Lazaro,
To have him find her here all ready.
᠌Aligi! Vienda di Giave!
Give up to her your bridal bedstead!
And all ye women, go and scatter wheat-
  grains, —
Upon her head the golden wheat-grains!
We'll come back ourselves here with music,
A little later and ask for the wine-jug.

[*The reaper jumps down and disappears
mid an outbreak of coarse laughter from the
others.*]

CHORUS OF REAPERS [*outside*]

Hand us out the wine-jug. That's the custom,
— The wine-jug, the wine-jug, and the woman!

[ALIGI *stands rigid, with his eyes fixed upon
the floor, perplexed, still holding in his hand
the mantle he has taken.*]

50

MILA

O innocence, O innocence, of all these
Young maidens here, you have heard not,
The filthiness, you have heard not,
Oh! Tell me you have heard not, heard not! —
At least not you, Ornella, oh, no, not
You who have wished to save me!

ANNA

Do not go near her, Ornella! Or would you
Have her ruin you? She, the daughter of the
    Sorcerer,
Must to every one bring ruin.

MILA

She comes to me because behind me
She sees here weeping the silent angel —
The guardian over my soul keeping vigil.

[ALIGI *turns quickly toward* MILA *at these
words, and gazes at her fixedly.*]

MARIA CORA

Oh! Oh! it is sacrilege! Sacrilege!

LA CINERELLA

Ha! She has blasphemed, she has blasphemed,
Against the heavenly angel.

FELAVIA

She will desecrate your hearthstone,
Candia, unless hence you chase her.

ANNA

Out with her, out, in good time, Aligi,
Seize her, and out to the dogs toss her!

LA CATALANA

Well I know you, Mila di Codra,
Well at Farne do they fear you,
And well I know your doings.
You brought death to Giovanna Cametra,
And death to the son of Panfilo.
You turned the head of poor Alfonso,
Gave Tillura the evil sickness,
Caused the death of your father, even,
Who now in damnation damns you!

MILA

May thou, God, protect his spirit

And unto peace his soul gather.
Ah! You it is who have blasphemed
Against a soul that is departed
And may your blaspheming speeches
Fall on you, whenever death fronts you!

[CANDIA, *seated on one of the chests, is sad
and silent. Now she rises, passes through the
restless circle of women, and advances toward
the persecuted one, slowly, without anger.*]

CHORUS OF REAPERS

Ahey! Ahey! How long to wait?
Have you come to an agreement?
— Oh, I say, shepherd, ho! you shepherd,
For yourself, then, do you keep her?
— Candia, what if Lazaro come back now?
— Is she then unwilling? But open,
Open! A hand we will lend her.
And meanwhile give us the wine-jug,
The wine-jug, the wine-jug's the custom!

[*Another reaper peers in through the
grating.*]

53

THE REAPER

Mila di Codra, come out here!
For you that will be much the better.
To try to escape us is useless,
We 'll seek now the oak-tree shady,
And throw dice for the one to have you,
That the chance for us all be equal,
Now, we will not quarrel for you,
As Lazaro did with Rainero,
No, we 'll have no useless bloodshed.
But, now, if you don't come out here,
Ere the last one turns up his dice-box,
Then this door we all shall break open
And carry things here with a free hand.
You are warned now; best heed this your
    warning,
Candia della Leonessa!

[*He jumps down and the clamor is much
abated. The ringing of the village church bells
can be heard in the distance.*]

CANDIA

Woman, hear me. Lo, I am the mother

54

Of these three innocent maidens,
Also of this youth, the bridegroom.
We were in peace in our home here,
In peace and in rest with God's favor,
And blessing with home rites the marriage,
You may see the wheat still in the baskets
And in the blest loaf the fresh flower!
You have entered in here and brought us
Suddenly conflict and sorrow,
Interrupted the kindred's giving,
In our hearts sowing thoughts of dark omen,
That have set my children weeping,
And my bowels yearn and weep with them.
All to chaff our good wheat grain is turning,
And a worse thing still may follow.
It is best for you to go now.
Go thou with God, knowing surely
He will help you, if you trust Him.
Oh! There is cause for all this our sorrow.
We would fain have desired your safety.
Yet now, turn your steps hence, swiftly,
So that none of this house need harm you.
The door, this my son will now open.

[*The victim listens in humility with bent head, pale and trembling.* ALIGI *steps toward the door and listens. His face shows great sorrow.*]

MILA

Christian mother, lo! the earth here
I kiss where your feet have trodden,
And I ask of you forgiveness,
With my heart in my hand lying,
In the palm of my hand, grieving,
For this sorrow of my bringing.
But I did not seek your dwelling:
I was blinded, with fear blinded,
And the Father, He, all-seeing,
Led me here thus to your fireside,
So that I, the persecuted,
Might find mercy by your fireplace,
Mercy making this day sacred.
O have mercy! Christian mother.
O have mercy! and each wheat grain
Resting here within these hampers
God will return a hundred-fold.

56

LA CATALANA [*whispering*]

Listen not. Whoever listens
Will be lost. The false one is she.
Oh! I know! Her father gave her,
To make her voice so sweet and gentle,
Evil roots of secret magic.

ANNA

Just see now how Aligi's spellbound!

MARIA CORA

Beware! beware! lest she give him
Fatal illness. O Lord, save us!
Have you not heard what all the reapers
Have been saying about Lazaro?

MONICA

Shall we stay here then till vespers
With these baskets on our heads thus?
I shall put mine on the ground soon.

[CANDIA *gazes intently upon her son, who is
fastened upon* MILA. *Suddenly fear and rage
seize her, and she cries aloud.*]

57

CANDIA

Begone, begone, you sorcerer's
Daughter! Go to the dogs! Begone!
In my house remain no longer!
Fling open the door, Aligi!

MILA

Mother of Ornella, — Love's own mother,
All, but not this, God forgiveth.
Trample on me, God forgiveth,
Cut off my hands, yet God forgiveth,
Gouge out my eyes, pluck my tongue out,
Tear me to shreds, yet God forgiveth,
Strangle me, yet God forgiveth,
But if you now (heed me, O heed me!
While the bells are ringing for Santo Gio-
    vanni).
If now you seize upon this body, —
This poor tortured flesh signed in Christ's
    name,
And toss it out there in that courtyard,
In sight of these your spotless daughters,
Abandoning it to sin of that rabble,

58

To hatred and to brutal lusting,
Then, O mother of Ornella,
Mother of innocence in so doing,
Doing that thing, God condemns you!

LA CATALANA

She was never christened, never,
Her father was never buried
In consecrated ground; under
A thorn-bush he lies. I swear it.

MILA

Demons are behind you, woman!
Black and foul and false your mouth is!

LA CATALANA

O Candia, hear her, hear her,
Curses heaping! But a little,
And she 'll drive you from your dwelling,
And then all the reapers threatened
Will most surely fall upon us.

ANNA DI BOVA

Up, Aligi! Drag her out there!

MARIA CORA

See you not how your Vienda,
Your young bride, looks like one dying?

LA CINERELLA

What kind of a man are you? Forsaken
Thus of all force in your muscles?
Is the tongue within your mouth, then,
Dried and shrivelled that you speak not?

FELAVIA

You seem lost. How then? Did your senses
Go astray afar off in the mountain? —
Did you lose your wits down in the valley?

MONICA

Look! He has n't let go of her mantle,
Since the time he took it from her.
To his fingers it seems rooted.

LA CATALANA

Do you think your son Aligi's
Mind is going? Heaven help us!

CANDIA

Aligi, Aligi! You hear me?
What ails you? Where are you? Gone are
    your senses?
What is coming to birth in your heart, son?

[*Taking the mantle out of his hand, she
throws it to the woman.*]

I myself will open the door; take her
And push her out of here straightway.
Aligi, to you I speak. You hear me?
Ah! verily you have been sleeping
For seven hundred hundred years,
And all of us are long forgotten.
Kindred! God wills my undoing.
I hoped these last days would bring solace
And that God would now give me repose,
That less bitterness now need I swallow;
But bitterness overpowers me.
My daughters! Take ye my black mantle
From out of the ancient chest there,
And cover my head and my sorrows,
Within my own soul be my wailing!

61

[*The son shakes his head, his face showing perplexity and sorrow, and he speaks as one in a dream.*]

ALIGI

What is your will of me, mother?
Unto you said I: " Ah! lay there
Against both of the door-posts the ploughshare,
The wain and the oxen, put sods there and
    stones there,
Yea, the mountain with all of its snow-drifts."
What did I say then?   And how answered
    you?
   " Heed the waxen cross that is holy,
That was blest on the Day of Ascension,
And the hinges with holy water sprinkled."
O, what is your will that I do?   It was night
    still
When she took the road that comes hither.
Profound, then, profound was my slumber,
O mother! although you had not mingled for
    me,
The wine with the seed of the poppy.
Now that slumber of Christ falls and fails me:

And though well I know whence this pro-
    ceedeth,
My lips are yet stricken with dumbness.
O woman! what then is your bidding?
That I seize her here now by her tresses, —
That I drag her out there in the courtyard, —
That I toss her for these dogs to raven?
Well! So be it! So be it! — I do so.

[ALIGI *advances toward* MILA, *but she
shrinks within the fireplace, clinging for
refuge.*]

MILA

Touch me not! Oh! you, you are sinning,
Against the old laws of the hearthstone —
You are sinning the great sin that's mortal
Against your own blood and the sanction
Of your race, of your own ancient kinfolk.
Lo! over the stone of the fireplace
I pour out the wine that was given
To me by your sister, in blood bound;
So now if you touch me, molest me,
All the dead in your land, in your country,

63

All those of the long years forgotten,
Generation to past generation,
That lie underground eighty fathoms
Will abhor you with horror eternal.

[*Taking the bowl of wine,* MILA *pours it
over the inviolate hearth. The women utter
fierce and frantic cries.*]

THE CHORUS OF KINDRED

O woe! She bewitches — bewitches the fire-
   place!
— She poured with the wine there a mixture.
I saw it, I saw her. 'T was stealthy!
— O take her, O take her, Aligi,
And force her away from the hearthstone.
— By the hair, O seize her, seize her!
— Aligi, fear you naught, fear nothing,
All her conjuring yet will be nothing.
— Take her away and shiver the wine-bowl!
Shiver it there against the andirons.
— Break the chain loose and engirdle
Her neck with it, three times twist it.

— She has surely bewitched the hearthstone.
— Woe! Woe for the house that totters!
Ah! What lamenting will here be lamented!

THE CHORUS OF REAPERS

Oho there! All quarrelling, are you?
We are waiting here and we 're watching.
We have cast the dice, we know the winner.
Bring her out to us, you shepherd!
Yes, yes! Or the door we 'll break down.

[*They join in blows on the door and in clamoring.*]

ANNA DI BOVA

Hold on! Hold on! and have patience a little,
But a little while longer, good menfolk.
Aligi is taking her. Soon you will have her.

[ALIGI, *like one demented, takes her by the wrists, but she resists and tries to free herself.*]

MILA

No! No! You are sinning, are sinning.
Crush under your feet my forehead

Or stun it with blows of your sheep-hook,
And when I am dead toss me out there.
No, no! God's punishment on you!
From the womb of your wife serpents
To you shall be born and brought forth.
You shall sleep no more, no more,
And rest shall forsake your eyelids,
From your eyes tears of blood shall gush forth.
Ornella, Ornella, defend me,
Aid me, O thou, and have mercy!
Ye sisters in Christ, do thou help me!

[*She frees herself and goes to the three sisters, who surround her. Blind with rage and horror,* ALIGI *lifts his hook to strike her on the head. Immediately his three sisters begin to cry and moan. This stops him at once; he lets the hook fall on his knees and with open arms he stares behind her.*]

ALIGI

Mercy of God! O give me forgiveness!
I saw the angel, silent, weeping.
He is weeping with you, O my sisters!

And at me he is gazing and weeping.
Even thus shall I see him forever,
Till the hour for my passing, yea! past it.
I have sinned thus against my own hearth-
    stone,
My own dead and the land of my fathers;
It will spurn me and scorn me forever,
Deny rest to my weary dead body!
For my sins, sisters, purification,
Seven times, seven times, I do ask it.
Seven days shall my lips touch the ashes,
And as many times more as the tears shed
From your gentle eyes, O my sisters!
Let the angel count them, my sisters,
And brand on my heart all their number!
It is thus that I ask you forgiveness.
Before God thus I ask you, my sisters,
Oh! pray you for brother Aligi,
Who must now return to the mountain.
And she who has suffered such shame here,
I pray you console her, refresh her
With drink, wipe the dust from her garments,
Bathe her feet with water and vinegar.

Comfort her! I wished not to harm her.
Spurred on was I by these voices.
And those who to this wrong have brought
  me
Shall suffer for many days greatly.
Mila di Codra! sister in Jesus,
O give me peace for my offences.
These flowerets of Santo Giovanni
Off from my sheep-hook now do I take them
And thus at your feet here I place them.
Look at you I cannot.   I 'm shamefaced.
Behind you I see the sad angel.
But this hand which did you offence here,
I burn in that fire with live embers.

   [*Dragging himself on his knees to the fireplace, he bends over and finds a burning ember.
Taking it with his left hand, he puts the point of
it in the palm of the right.*]

MILA

It is forgiven.   No, no.   Do not wound
  yourself.
For me, I forgive you, and God shall receive

68

"O GIVE ME PEACE FOR MY OFFENCES."

Act I., Page 68.

Your penitent prayer. Rise up from the fire-
    place!
One only, God only may punish;
And He that hand hath given to you
To guide your flocks to the pasture.
And how then your sheep can you pasture
If your hand is infirm, O Aligi?
For me, in all humbleness, I forgive you,
And your name I shall ever remember,
Morn, eve, and midday shall my blessing
Follow you with your flocks in the mountains.

THE CHORUS OF REAPERS [*outside*]

— Oho, there! Oho, there! How now?
— What is the row? Do you fool us?
— Ho! We 'll tear down the door there.
— Yes, yes! Take that timber, the plough-
    beam.
— Shepherd, we 'll not have you fool us.
Now, now, that iron there, take it!
Down with it! Crash down the door there!
— Ho, shepherd Aligi! Now answer!
One, then! Two! Three, and down goes it!

69

[*The heavy breathing of the men lifting the timber and iron is heard.*]

ALIGI

For you, for me, and for all my people,
I make the sign of the cross!

[*Rising and going toward the door, he continues.*]

Reapers of Norca! This door I open.

[*The men answer in a unanimous clamor. The wind brings the sound of the bells.* ALIGI *draws the bars and bolts and silently crosses himself, then he takes down from the wall the cross of wax and kisses it.*]

Women, God's servants, cross yourselves
    praying.

[*All the women cross themselves and kneeling murmur the litany.*]

WOMEN [together]

Kyrie eleison!

Lord have mercy upon us!

70

Christe eleison!

      Christ have mercy upon us!

Kyrie eleison!

      Lord have mercy upon us!

Christe audi nos!

      O Christ hear us!

Christe exaudi nos!

      O Christ hearken unto us!

[*The shepherd then lays the cross on the threshold between the hoe and the distaff and opens the door. In the yard glittering in the fierce sun the linen-clad reapers appear.*]

ALIGI

Brothers in Christ! Behold the cross
That was blest on the Day of Ascension!
I have placed it there on the threshold,
That you may not sin against this gentle
Lamb of Christ who here finds refuge,
Seeking safety in this fireplace.

[*The reapers, struck silent and deeply impressed, uncover their heads.*]

71

I saw there standing behind her
The angel who guards her, silent,
These eyes that shall see life eternal
Saw her angel that stood there weeping.
Look, brothers in Christ, I swear it!
Turn back to your wheat-fields and reap
    them,
Harm you not one who has harmed you never!
Nor let the false enemy beguile you
Any longer with his potions.
Reapers of Norca, heaven bless you!
May the sheaves in your hands be doubled!
And may Santo Giovanni's head severed
Be shown unto you at the sunrise,
If, for this, to-night you ascend the hill Plaia.
And wish ye no harm unto me, the shepherd,
To me, Aligi, our Saviour's servant!

    [*The kneeling women continue the litanies,*
CANDIA *invoking, the others responding.*]

CANDIA and CHORUS OF THE KINDRED

Mater purissima,   Mother of Purity,
   ora pro nobis.   pray for us.

Mater castissima,	Mother of Chastity,
ora pro nobis.	pray for us.
Mater inviolata,	Mother Inviolate,
ora pro nobis.	pray for us.

[*The reapers bow themselves, touch the cross with their hands and then touch their lips and silently withdraw toward the glittering fields outside,* ALIGI *leaning against the jamb of the door following with his eyes their departure, the silence meanwhile broken only by voices coming from the country pathways outside.*]

FIRST VOICE

O! turn back, Lazaro di Roio.

ANOTHER VOICE

Turn back, turn back, Lazaro!

[*The shepherd, startled and shading his face with his hands, looks toward the path.*]

CANDIA and THE WOMEN

Virgo veneranda,	Virgin venerated,
Virgo predicanda,	Virgin admonishing,
Virgo potens,	Virgin potential,
ora pro nobis.	pray for us.

ALIGI

Father, father, what is this?   Why are you
  bandaged?
Why are you bleeding, father?   Speak out and
  tell me,
O ye men of the Lord!   Who wounded him?

[LAZARO *appears at the door with his head
bandaged, two men in white linen supporting
him.*   CANDIA *stops praying, rises to her feet
and goes to the entrance.*]

ALIGI

Father, halt there!   The cross lies there on the
  door-sill,
You cannot pass through without kneeling
  down.
If this blood be unjust blood you cannot pass
  through.

[*The two men sustain the tottering man
and he falls guiltily on his knees outside the
doorway.*]

74

CANDIA

O daughters, my daughters, 't was true then!
O weep, my daughters! let mourning enfold
  us!

[*The daughters embrace their mother. The
kindred before rising put their hampers down
on the ground.* MILA *takes up her mantle and
still kneeling wraps herself up in it, hiding her
face. Almost creeping, she approaches the
door toward the jamb opposite that where*
ALIGI *leans. Silently and swiftly she rises and
leans against the wall, and stands there wrapt
and motionless, watching her chance to disappear.*]

Act II.

A MOUNTAIN *cavern is seen partially protected by rough boards, straw, and twigs and opening wide upon a stony mountain path. From the wide opening are seen green pastures, snow-clad peaks, and passing clouds. In the cavern are pallets made of sheep-pelts, small, rude wooden tables, pouches and skins, filled and empty, a rude bench for wood turning and carving, with an axe upon it, a draw-knife, plane, rasps, and other tools, and near them finished pieces; distaffs, spoons and ladles, mortars and pestles, musical instruments, and candlesticks. A large block of the trunk of a walnut tree has at its base the bark, and above, in full relief, the figure of an angel hewn into shape to the waist, with the two wings almost finished. Before the image of the Virgin in a depression of the cavern like a niche, a lamp is burning. A shepherd's bag-*

76

pipe hangs close by. The bells of the sheep wandering in the stillness of the mountain may be heard. The day is closing and it is about the time of the autumnal equinox.

The treasure-seeker, Malde, *and* Anna Onna, *the old herb-gatherer, are lying asleep on the pelts, in their rags.* Cosma, *the saint, dressed in a long friar's frock, is also asleep, but in a sitting posture with his arms clasped about his knees and his chin bowed over on them.* Aligi *is seated on a little bench, intent upon carving with his tools the walnut block.* Mila di Codra *is seated opposite, gazing at him.*

MILA

Bided mute the patron angel
From the walnut woodblock carven,
Deaf the wood stayed, secret, sacred,
Saint Onofrio vouchsafed nothing.

Till said one apart, a third one
(O have pity on us, Patron!)
Till said one apart, the fair one,
Lo! my heart all willing, waiting!

77

Would he quaff a draught of marvel?
Let him take my heart's blood, quaff it!
But of this make no avowal,
But of this make no revealing.

Suddenly the stump budded branches,
Out of the mouth a branch sprang budding,
Every finger budded branches,
Saint Onofrio all grew green again!

[*She bends over to gather the chips and
shavings around the carved block.*]

ALIGI

O Mila, this too is hewn from the stump of
    a walnut,
Grow green will it, Mila? — Grow green
    again?

MILA [*still bent over*]

"Would he quaff a draught of marvel
Let him take my heart's blood." —

ALIGI

Grow green will it, Mila? — Grow green
    again?

MILA

" But of this make no avowal,
But of this make no revealing."

ALIGI

Mila, Mila, let a miracle now absolve us!
And may the mute patron angel grant us
    protection.
'T is for him that I work, but not with my
    chisel,
Ah! for him do I work with my soul in my
    fingers!
But what are you seeking? What have you
    lost there?

MILA

I but gather the shavings, that in fire we burn
    them
With each a grain of pure incense being added.
Make haste, then, Aligi, for the time is
    nearing.
The moonlight of September fleeting, lessen-
    ing;

All of the shepherds now are leaving, depart-
    ing,
Some on to Puglia fare, some Romeward
    faring; —
And whither then will my love his footsteps
    be turning?
Wherever he journeys still may his pathway
Go facing fresh pastures and springs, not
    winds keen and chilling,
And of me may he think when the night over-
    takes him!

ALIGI

Romeward faring then shall go Aligi,
Onward to Rome whither all roads are leading,
His flock along with him to lofty Rome,
To beg an indulgence of the Vicar,
Of the Holy Vicar of Christ our Saviour,
For he of all shepherds is the Shepherd.
Not to Puglia land will go Aligi,
But to our blest Lady of Schiavonia,
Sending to her by Alai of Averna
These two candlesticks of cypress wood, only,

80

And with them merely two humble tapers,
So she forget not a lowly sinner
She, our Lady, who guardeth the sea-shore.
Then when this angel shall be all finished,
Aligi upon a mule's back will load it,
And step by step will he wend on with it.

MILA

O hasten, O hasten! for the time is ripening.
From the girdle downward very nearly
Sunk in the wood yet and lost is the angel;
The feet are held fast in the knots, the hands
    without fingers,
The eyes with the forehead still level.
You hastened indeed his wings to give him,
Feather by feather, yet forth he flies not!

ALIGI

Gostanzo will aid me in this, the painter,
Gostanzo di Bisegna; the painter is he
Who tells stories on wood in color.
Unto him I have spoken already,
And he will give unto me fine colors.

81

Perhaps, too, the good monks at the abbey,
For a yearling, a little fine gold leaf
For the wings and the bosom will give me.

MILA

O hasten! Hasten! The time is rip'ning,
Longer than day is the night already,
From the valley the shades rise more quickly,
And unawares they shut down around us.
Soon the eye will guide the hand no longer,
And unsuccored of art will grope the blind
  chisel!

[COSMA *stirs in his sleep and moans. From
a distance the sacred songs of pilgrims crossing
the mountain are heard.*]

Cosma is dreaming. Who knows what he 's
  dreaming!
Listen, listen, the songs of the pilgrims
Who across the mountain go journeying,
May be to Santa Maria della Potenza,
Aligi, — toward your own country, — toward
Your own home, where your mother is sitting.

And may be they will pass by very near,
And your mother will hear, and Ornella,
Mayhap, and they 'll say: " These must be
    pilgrims
Coming down from the place of the shepherds;
And yet no loving token is sent us! "

[ALIGI *is bending over his work carving
the lower part of the block. Giving a blow
with the axe he leaves the iron in the wood and
comes forward anxiously.*]

ALIGI

Ah! Why, why will you touch where the heart
    is hurting?
Oh! Mila, I will speed on, overtake their cross-
    bearer
And beg him bear onward my loving thoughts
    with them.
And yet, Mila, yet — Oh! how shall I say it,
    Mila?

MILA

You will say: " O good cross-bearer, I prithee,
If ye cross through the valley of San Biagio,

83

Through the countryside called Acquanova,
Ask ye there for the house of a woman
Who is known as Candia della Leonessa,
And stay ye your steps there, for there most
    surely
Drink shall ye have to restore you, and may be
Much beside given.   Then stay there and say ye:
' Aligi, your son, sends unto you greeting,
And to his sisters, and also the bride, Vienda,
And he promises he will be coming
To receive from your hands soon your blessing
Ere in peace he depart on long travels.
And he says, too, that he is set free now,
From her — the evil one — during these late
    days;
And he will be cause of dissension no longer,
And he will be cause of lamenting no longer,
To the mother, the bride, and the sisters.' "

ALIGI

Mila, Mila, what ill wind strikes you
And stirs up your soul in you thus? — A wind
    sudden,

A wind full of fearing!   And on your lips
    dying,
Your voice is; your blood your cheek is drain-
    ing.
And wherefore, tell me, should I be sending
This message of falsehood to my mother?

MILA

It is the truth, it is the truth, I tell you,
O brother mine and dear to the sister,
It is true what I say; as true is it
That I have remained by you untainted,
Like a sacred lamp before your faith burning,
With immaculate love before you shining.
It is the truth, it is the truth I tell you.
And I say: Go, go, speed ye on your pathway
And meet ye the cross-bearer so that he carry
Your greetings of peace on to Acquanova.
Now come is the hour of departure
For the daughter of Jorio.   And let it be so.

ALIGI

Yea, verily, you have partaken of honey, wild
    honey

85

That your mind is thus troubled!
And you would go whither? Oh, whither,
  Mila?

MILA

Pass on thither where all roads are leading.

ALIGI

Ah! Will you come then with me? O, come
  with me!
Though full long the journey, you also, Mila,
Will I place on the mule's back and travel,
Cherishing hope, toward Rome the eternal!

MILA

Needs be that I go the opposite way,
With steps hurried, bereft of all hoping.

ALIGI [*turning impatiently to the sleeping old herb-woman*]

Anna Onna! Up, arouse you! Go and find
  me
Grains of black hellebore, hellebore ebon,
To give back to this woman her senses.

MILA

O be not angry, Aligi, for if you are angry —
For if you are also against me, how shall I
    live through
This day till the evening? For behold, if you
    trample
My heart beneath you, I shall gather it never
    again!

ALIGI

And I to my home shall be turning never
    again,
If not with you, O daughter of Jorio,
Mila di Codra, my own by the Sacrament!

MILA

Aligi, can I cross the very threshold
Whereon once the waxen cross was lying,
Where a man once appeared who was bloody?
And unto whom said the son of this man:
" If this blood be unjust blood you cannot
    pass through "?
High noonday 't was then, the eve of the day
Of Santo Giovanni, and harvest day.

87

Now in peace on that wall hangs the idle
    sickle;

Now at rest lies the grain in the granary;

But of that sorrow's sowing the seeds are still
    growing.

[COSMA *moves in his sleep and moans.*]

ALIGI

Know you, then, one who shall lead you by the
    hand thither!

COSMA [*crying out in his sleep*]

O do not unbind him! No, no, do not unbind
    him!

[*The saint, stretching his arms, lifts up his
face from his knees.*]

MILA

Cosma, Cosma, what are you dreaming? Tell
    your dreaming!

[COSMA *wakens and rises.*]

ALIGI

What have you been seeing? Tell your seeing!

88

COSMA

The face of Fear was turned full upon me.
I have beheld it. But I may not tell it.
Every dream that cometh of God must be
    chastened
From the fire of it first before giving.
I have beheld it. And I shall speak, surely.
Yet not now, lest I speak the name vainly
Of my Lord and my God, lest I judge now
While my darkness is still overpowering.

ALIGI

O Cosma, thou art holy. Many a year
Have you bathed in the melting snow water,
In the water o'erflowing the mountain,
Quenching your thirst in the clear sight of
    Heaven,
And this day you have slept in my cavern,
On the sheep-skin that's steamed well in
    sulphur
So the spirit of evil must shun it.
In your dreaming now you have seen visions,
And the eye of the Lord God is on you.

Help me then with your sure divination!
Now to you I shall speak. You will answer.

COSMA

All unready am I in wisdom,
Nor have I, O youth, understanding
Of so much as the stone in the path of the
    shepherd.

ALIGI

O Cosma, man of God, heed me and listen!
I implore by the angel in that block enfolded,
Who has no ears to hear and yet heareth!

COSMA

Simple words speak ye, O shepherd,
And repose not your trust in me,
But in the holy truth only.

    [MALDE *and* ANNA ONNA *awaken and lean
upon their elbows listening.*]

ALIGI

Cosma, this, then, is the holy truth:
I turned from the mountain and Puglia valley

90

With my flock on the day Corpus Domini,
And after I found for my flock good shelter
I went to my home for my three days' resting.
And I find there in my house my mother
Who says unto me: " Son of mine, a com-
    panion
For you have I found." Then say I:
    " Mother,
I ever obey your commandments." She an-
    swered:
" 'T is well. And lo! here is the woman."
We were espoused. And the kindred gathered,
Escorting the bride to our threshold.
Aloof I stood like a man on the other
Bank of a river, seeing all things as yonder,
Afar, past the water flowing between,
The water that flows everlastingly.
Cosma, this was on a Sunday. And mingled
With my wine was no seed of the poppy.
Why then, notwithstanding, did slumber pro-
    found
My heart all forgetting o'erpower?
I believe I slept years seven hundred.

91

We awoke on the Monday belated.
Then the loaf of the Bridal my mother
Broke over the head of a weeping virgin.
Untouched had she lain by me. The kindred
Came then with their wheat in their hampers.
But mute stayed I wrapped up in great
    sadness.
As one in the shadow of death I was dwelling.
Behold now! on a sudden, all trembling,
There appeared in our doorway this woman,
Hard pursuing and pressing her, reapers, —
Hounds! that wanted to seize her and have her.
Then implored she and pleaded for safety.
But not even one of us, Cosma,
Moved, except one, my sister, the littlest,
Who dared rush to the door and bar it.
And lo, now by those dogs was it shaken,
With uttering of curses and threat'ning.
And in hatred against this sad creature
Were their foul mouths unleashed and barking.
To the pack would the women have tossed her,
But she trembling still by the hearthstone,
Was pleading us not to make sacrifice of her.

I, too, myself, seized her with hatred and
    threat'ning,
Though it seemed to me, then, I was drag-
    ging
At my own very heart, the heart of my child-
    hood.
She cried out, and above her head I lifted
My sheep-hook to strike her.
                            Then wept my sisters!
Then behind her beheld I the angel weeping!
With these eyes, O saint, the angel watching
    and weeping mutely.
                        Down on my knees fell I,
Imploring forgiveness.   And then to punish
This, my hand, I took up from the fireplace
A burning ember.
                        " No, do not burn it,"
She cried aloud, — this woman cried to me.
— O Cosma! saint holy, with waters from
    snow-peaks
Purified are you, dawning by dawning;
You, too, woman, who know all herbs growing
For the healing of flesh that is mortal,

Yea, all virtue of roots that are secret;
— Malde, you, too, with that branch of yours
forking
May fathom where treasure is hidden,
Entombed at the feet of the dead now dead
For a hundred years, or a thousand — true is
it? —
In the depths of the depths of the heart of the
mountain.
Of ye then, I ask, of ye who can hear
The deep things within that come from afar,
Whence came that voice, — O from what far
distance
That came and that spake so Aligi should
hear it?
(Oh, answer ye me!) — When she said unto
me:
" And how then your flocks can you pasture
If your hand is infirm, O Aligi? "
Ah! with these her words did she gather
My soul from my body within me,
Even as you, O woman, gather your simples!

[MILA *weeps silently.*]

ANNA ONNA

There 's an herb that is red and called Glaspi,
And another is white called Egusa,
And the one and the other grow up far
    apart,
But their roots grope together and meet
Underneath the blind earth, and entwine
So closely that sever them never could ever
Santa Lucia. Their leaves are diverse,
But one and the same is their seven years'
    flower.
But all this is their record in records.
It is Cosma who knoweth the power of the
    Lord.

ALIGI

Heed me then, Cosma! The slumber of for-
    getfulness
Was by Commandment sent to my pillow.
By whom? Closed by the hand of Innocence
Was the door of Safety. Came to me the
    apparition —
The Angel of Counsel. And out of the
    word

95

Of her mouth was created the pledge eternal.
Who then was my wife, before ever
Good wheat, holy loaf, or fair flower?

COSMA

O shepherd Aligi! God's are the just steel-
yards of Justice.
God's only is the just balance of Justice.
Notwithstanding, O take ye counsel,
From the Angel of Counsel, who gave you
your surety.
Yea, take pledge of him for this stranger.
But she left untouched, where is she?

ALIGI

For the sheepstead I left after vespers,
On the eve of Santo Giovanni.

At daybreak
I found myself wending above Capracinta.
On the crest I awaited the sunrise,
And I saw in the disc of its blazing
The bleeding head that was severed.

To my sheepfold

Then came I,—and again I began — guarding
　　my sheep — to suffer
For me seemed that sleep still overwhelmed me,
And my flock on my life's force was browsing.
Oh! why still was my heart heavy laden?
O Cosma! first saw I the shadow,
Then the figure, there, there, at the entrance,
On the morning of San Teobaldo.
On the rock out there was sitting this woman,
And she did not arise for she could not,
So sore were her feet and bleeding.
　　　　　　　　Said she: "Aligi,
Do you know me? "
　　　　　　　　I answered: " Thou art Mila."
And no word more we spoke, for no more
　　were we
Twain.　Nor on that day were contaminated
Nor after, ever.
　　　　　　　I speak but the truth.

COSMA

O shepherd Aligi!　You have verily lighted
A holy lamp in your darkness.

Yet it is not enkindled in limits appointed,
Chosen out of old time by your fathers.
You have moved farther off the Term Sacred.
How then if the lamp were spent and were
    quenched?
For wisdom is in man's heart a well-spring
Profound; but only the pure man may draw
    of its waters.

ALIGI

Now pray I great God that He place upon
    us
The seal of the Sacrament eternal!
See ye this that I do? Not hand but soul
Is carving this wood in the similitude
Of the Angel apparition. I began
On the Day of Assumption. Rosary time
Shall it be finished. This my design is:
On to Rome with my flock I shall wander,
And along with me carry my Angel,
On mule-back laden. I will go to the Holy
    Father,
In the name of San Pietro Celestino,

OF JORIO

Who upon Mount Morrone did penance.
I shall go to the Shepherd of shepherds,
With this votive offering, humbly imploring
Indulgence, that the bride, yet untouched, may
    return
To her mother, set free thus and blameless;
Then as mine I may cherish this stranger,
Who knows well how to weep all unheeded.
So now I ask this of your deep-reaching wis-
    dom,
Cosma; will this grace unto me be conceded?

COSMA

All the ways of mankind appear the direct
    ways
To man: but the Lord God is weighing heart-
    secrets.
High the walls, high the walls of man's strong-
    hold,
Huge are its portals of iron; and around and
    around it
Heavy the shade of tombs where grass grows
    pallid.

Let not your lamb browse upon that grass
  grown pallid,
O shepherd Aligi, best question the mother.

A VOICE [*calling outside*]

Cosma, Cosma! If you are within, come forth!

COSMA

Who is calling for me? Did you hear a voice
  calling?

THE VOICE

Come forth, Cosma, by the blood that is
  holy!
O Christian brothers, the sign of the cross
  make ye!

COSMA

Behold me. Who calls me? Who wants me?

[*At the mouth of the cavern two shepherds
appear, wearing sheep-skin coats, holding a
gaunt and sickly youth whose arms are bound
to his body with several turns of a rope.*]

100

FIRST SHEPHERD

O Christian brothers!   The sign of the cross
    make ye!
May the Lord from the enemy keep you!
And to guard well the door say a prayer.

SECOND SHEPHERD

O Cosma, this youth is possessed of a demon.
Now for three days the devil has held him.
Behold, O behold how he tortures him now.
He froths at the mouth, turning livid and
    shrieking.
With strong ropes we needed to tie and bind
    him
To bring him to you.   You who freed before
    now
Bartolomeo dei Cionco ala Petrara, do you,
O wise man of mercy, do you this one
    also
Liberate!   Force now the demon to leave
    him!
O chase him away from him, cure him and heal
    him!

COSMA

What is his name and the name of his father?

FIRST SHEPHERD

Salvestro, di Mattia di Simeone.

COSMA

Salvestro, how then, you will to be healed?
Be of good heart, my son, O be trustful!
Lo! I say unto you, fear not!

                    And ye
Wherefore have ye bound him? Let him be
   free!

SECOND SHEPHERD

Come with us then to the chapel, Cosma.
There we can let him be free. He would flee
   away, here.
He is frantic always, for escape ever ready.
And sudden to take it. He's frothing. Come
   on then!

COSMA

That will I, God helping. Be of good heart,
   my son!

102

[*The two shepherds carry the youth off.*
MALDE *and* ANNA ONNA *follow them for
awhile, then halt, gazing after them,* MALDE
*with a forked olive branch with a small ball of
wax stuck on at the larger end, the old woman
leaning on her crutch and with her bag of
simples hanging in front.   Finally they also
disappear from sight.   The saint from the
doorway turns back toward his host.*]

COSMA

I go in God's peace, shepherd Aligi.
For the comfort I found in your cavern,
May you be blessèd!   Lo! now they called
unto me
And therefore I answered.   Before you may
enter
Upon your new way, the old laws well consider.
Who will change the old ways shall be win-
nowed.
See ye guard well your father's commandment.
See ye heed well your mother's instruction.
Hold them ever steadfast in your bosom.

103

And God guide your feet, that you may not
    be taken
In lariats nor into live embers stumble!

ALIGI

Cosma, quite well have you heard me? That
    I remain sinless.
Never I tainted myself but kept good faith,
Quite well have you heard of the sign God
    Almighty
Has revealed me and sent here unto me?
I await what will come, my flesh mortifying.

COSMA

I say unto you: Best question your parents
Ere you lead to your roof-tree this stranger.

A VOICE [calling from outside]

Cosma, don't delay longer! Surely 't will kill
    him.

COSMA [turning to MILA]

Peace unto you, woman! If good be within
    you

Let it pour forth from you like tears falling
Without being heard. I may soon return.

ALIGI

I come. I follow. Not all have I told you.

MILA

Aligi, 't is true: not all are you telling!
Go to the roadside. The cross-bearer watch
    for
And implore him to carry the message.

[*The saint goes off over the pasture land.
The singing of the pilgrims is heard from time
to time.*]

MILA

Aligi, Aligi: Not all did we tell!
Yet better it were that my mouth were choked
    up,
Better that stones and that ashes
Held me speechless. Hear then this only
From me, Aligi. I have done you no evil;
And none shall I do you. Healed and re-
    stored now

105

Are my feet.   And I know well the path-
ways.
Now arrived is the hour of departure
For the daughter of Jorio.   Now then so be it!

ALIGI

I know not, you know not what hour may be
coming.
Replenish the oil in our lamp of the Virgin,
Take the oil from the skin.   Some yet is within
And wait for me here.   I seek the cross-bearer,
Right well what to say unto him know I.

MILA

Aligi, brother of mine!   Give me your hand,
now!

ALIGI

Mila, the road is but there, not far away.

MILA

Give me that hand of yours, so I may kiss it.
'T is the drop that I yield to my thirst.

106

ALIGI [*coming closer*]

With the ember I wanted to burn it, Mila,
This sinful hand that sought to offend you.

MILA

All that I forget. I am only the woman
You found on the rock there seated,
By who knows what roads coming hither!

ALIGI [*coming again close*]

Upon your face your tears are not drying,
Dear woman. A tear is now staying
On the eyelashes, while you speak trembles,
    and falls not.

MILA

Over us hovers deep stillness. Aligi, just
    listen!
Hushed is the singing. With the grasses and
    snow-peaks
We are alone, brother mine, we are alone.

ALIGI

Mila, now you are unto me as you first
    were

107

Out there on the rock, when you were all
    smiling,
With your eyes all shining, your feet all bleed-
    ing.

MILA

And you, — you, — are you not now the one
    who was kneeling, —
Who the flowrets of Santo Giovanni
Put down on the ground? Ah! by one were
    they gathered
Who bears them yet, wears them yet — in her
    scapulary.

ALIGI

Mila, there is in your voice a vibration
That while it consoles me, it saddens.
As even October, when, all my flocks with me,
I border the bordering stretches of seashore.

MILA

To border them with you, the shore and the
    mountain
Ah! I would that that fate were my fate ever-
    more.

ALIGI

O my love, be preparing for such wayfaring!
Though the road there be long, for that is
Love strong.

MILA

Aligi, I 'd pass there through fires ever flam-
ing,
Onward still wending by roads never ending.

ALIGI

To cull on the hill-top the blue gentian lonely,
On the seashore only the star-fish flower.

MILA

There on my knees would I drag myself on,
Placing them down on the tracks you were
marking.

ALIGI

Think, too, of the places to rest when the night
should o'ertake us,
And the mint and the thyme that would be
your pillows.

109

MILA

I cannot think. No. Yet give leave this one
    night more
That I live with you, here, where you are here
    breathing,
That I hear you asleep and be with you,
And over you keep, like your dogs, faithful
    vigil!

ALIGI

O, you know, O, you know what must await us.
How with you must I ever divide the bread,
    salt, and water.
And so shall I share with you also the pallet,
Unto death and eternity. Give me your hands!

    [*They grasp each other's hands, gazing
into each other's eyes.*]

MILA

Ah! we tremble, we tremble. You are frigid,
Aligi. You are blanching. O whither
Is flowing the blood your face loses?

    [*She frees herself and touches his face with
both hands.*]

110

MILA DI CODRA AND ALIGI.

Act II., Page 111.

ALIGI

O Mila, Mila, I hear a great thundering,
All the mountain is shaking and sinking,
Where are you? Where are you? All is
  veiled.

[*He stretches out his hand toward her as
one tottering. They kiss each other. They
fall down upon their knees, facing each other.*]

MILA

Have mercy upon us, blessed Virgin!

ALIGI

Have mercy upon us, O Christ Jesus!

[*A deep silence follows.*]

A VOICE [*outside*]

Shepherd, ho! You are wanted, and in a
  hurry.
A black sheep has broken his shank.

[ALIGI *rises totteringly and goes toward
the entrance.*]

111

You are wanted at once and must hurry,
And there is a woman I know not.
On her head is a basket. For you she is asking.

[ALIGI *turns his head and looks toward*
MILA *with an all-embracing glance. She is
still on her knees.*]

ALIGI [*in a whisper*]

Mila, replenish the oil in our lamp of the
    Virgin,
So it go not out. See, it barely is burning.
Take the oil from the skin. Some yet is within.
And await me. I only must go to the sheep-
    fold.
Fear nothing, for God is forgiving.
Because we trembled will Mary forgive us.
Replenish the oil and pray her for mercy.

[*He goes out into the fields.*]

MILA

O Holy Virgin! Grant me this mercy:
That I may stay here with my face to earth
    bowed,

112

Cold here, that I may be found dead here,

That I may be removed hence for burial.

No trespass there was in thine eyesight.

No trespass there was. For Thou unto us
    wert indulgent.

The lips did no trespass. (To bear witness

There wert Thou!) The lips did no trespass.

So under Thine eyes I may die here, die here!

For strength have I none to leave here, O
    Mother!

Yet remain with him here Mila cannot!

Mother clement! I was never sinful,

But a well-spring tramped on and trodden.

Shamed have I been in the eyes of Heaven,

But who took away from my memory

This shame of mine if not Thou, Mary?

Born anew then was I when love was born
    in me.

Thou it was willed it, O faithful Virgin!

All the veins of this new blood spring from
    afar,

Spring from far off, from the far, far away,

From the depths of the earth where she rests,

113

She who nourished me once in days long ago,
    long ago.

Let it also be she who bears now for me
    witness

Of innocency! Madonna, Thou also bore
    witness!

The lips did no trespass here now (Thou wert
    witness),

No, there was none in the lips, no, in the lips
    there was none.

And if I trembled, O let me bear that tres-
    pass,

Bear ever that tremor with me beyond!

Here I close up within me my eyes with my
    fingers.

    [*With the index and middle finger of each
hand she presses her eyes, bowing her head to
the earth.*]

Death do I feel. Now do I feel it draw closer.

The tremor increaseth. Yet not the heart
    ceaseth.

                [*Rising impetuously.*]

Ah, wretch that I am, that which was told me
To do, I did not, though thrice did he say it:
" Replenish the oil." And lo! now 't is dying!

[*She goes toward the oil-skin hanging from
a beam, with her eye still watching the dying
flame, endeavoring to keep it alive with the
murmured prayer:*]

Ave Maria, gratia plena, Dominus tecum.
(Hail, Mary, full of grace, the Lord be with
   thee.)

[*Opening the skin, it flattens in her hands.
She searches for the flask to draw off the oil,
but is able to get but one or two drops.*]

'T is empty! 'T is empty! But three drops,
   Virgin,
For my unction extreme prithee be given me,
But two for my hands, for my lips the other,
And all for my soul, all the three!
For how can I live when back he returns here,
What can I say, Mother, what can I say?
Surely then he will see, or ere he see me,
How the lamp has gone out. If my loving

Sufficed not to keep the flame burning,
How pale unto him will this love of mine,
    Mother, appear!

[*Again she tries the skin, looking again for
other receptacles, upsetting everything and
still murmuring prayers.*]

Cause it to burn, O Mother intrepid!
But a little while longer, as much longer only
As an Ave Maria, a Salve
Regina, O Mother of Mercy, of Pity!

[*In the frenzy of her search she goes to
the entrance and hears a step and catches sight
of a shadow.   She calls aloud.*]

O woman, good woman, Christian sister,
Come you hither! and may the Lord bless you!
Come you hither!   For mayhap the Lord sends
    you.
What bear you in your basket?   If a little
Oil, oh, then of your charity, give me a little!
Pray enter and take of all these your free
    choice,
These ladles, spindles, mortars, distaffs, any!

116

For need that there is here for Our Lady,
To replenish the oil in her lamp there hanging
And not to quench it; if through me it be
    quenched,
I shall lose sight of the way to Heaven.
Christian woman, grasp you my meaning?
Will you to me do this loving kindness?

[*The woman appears at the entrance, her
head and face covered with a black mantle.
She takes down the basket from her head without a word and placing it on the ground re-
moves the cloth, takes out the phial of oil and
offers it to* MILA.]

MILA

Ah! be thou blessèd, be thou blessèd! Lord
    God
Reward thee on earth, and in Heaven also!
You have some! You have some! In mourn-
    ing are you;
But the Madonna will grant it to you
To see again the face of your lost one, —
All for this deed of your charity done me.

117

[*She takes the phial and turns anxiously to go to the dying lamp.*]

Ah! perdition upon me!   'T is quenched.

[*The phial falls from her hand and breaks. For a few seconds she remains motionless, stunned with the terrible omen. The woman leaning down to the spilled oil touches it with her fingers and crosses herself. MILA regards the woman with utter sadness and the resignation of despair makes her voice hollow and slow.*]

MILA

Pardon me, pardon, Christian pilgrim,
This your charity turned to nothing.
The oil wasted, broken in pieces the phial,
Misfortune upon me befallen.
Tell me what choose you?   All these things here
Were fashioned out thus by the shepherd.
A new distaff and with it a spindle
Wish you?   Or wish you a mortar and pestle?
Tell me, I pray.   For nothing know I any
     more.
I am one of the lost in the earth beneath.

OF JORIO

THE CLOAKED ONE

Daughter of Jorio! I have come unto you,
To you, bringing here, thus, this basket,
So I a boon may beseech of you.

MILA

Ah! heavenly voice that I ever
In the deeps of my soul have been hearing!

THE CLOAKED ONE

To you come I from Acquanova.

MILA

Ornella, Ornella art thou!

[ORNELLA *uncovers her face.*]

ORNELLA

The sister am I of Aligi;
The daughter am I of Lazaro.

MILA

I kiss your two feet with humility,
That have carried you here to me

119

So that again your dear face I behold
This hour, this last hour of my mortal suf-
fering.
To give me pity you were the first one,
You are now, too, the last one, Ornella!

ORNELLA

If I was the first, penitence
Great I have suffered. I am telling
The truth to you, Mila di Codra.
And still is my suffering bitter.

MILA

Oh! your voice in its sweetness is quivering.
In the wound doth the knife that hurts quiver.
And much more, ah! more doth it quiver
And you do not yet know that, Ornella!

ORNELLA

If only you knew this my sorrow!
If only you knew how much sadness
The small kindness I did for you caused me!
From my home that is left desolated
I come, where we weep and are perishing.

MILA

Why thus are you vested in mourning?
Who is dead then? You do not answer.
Mayhap — mayhap — the newly come sister?

ORNELLA

Ah! She is the one you wish perished!

MILA

No, no. God is my witness. I feared it,
And the fear of it seized me within me.
Tell me, tell me. Who is it? Answer,
For God's sake and for your own soul's sake!

ORNELLA

Not one of us yet has been taken;
But all of us there are still mourning
The dear one who leaves us abandoned
And gives himself up to his ruin.
If you could behold the forsaken one,
If our mother you could but behold,
You would quiver indeed. Unto us
Come is the Summer of blackness, come is

121

The Autumn bitter, oppressive,
And never a circling twelvemonth's season
Could be unto us so saddening. Surely,
When I shut to the door to help you and save
  you
And gave myself up to my ruin,
You did not then seem to me so unfeeling, —
You who implored for compassion's sake, —
You who sought my name of me
That you might in your blessings whisper it!
But since then my name is shadowed in shame.
Every night, every day in our household,
I am railed upon, shunned, cast away.
They single me out. They, pointing, cry out:
"Lo! that is the one, behold her,
Who put up the bars of the entrance
So that evil within might stay safely
And hide at its ease by the hearthstone."
I cannot stay longer. Thus say I: " Far rather
Hew at me, all, with your knife-blades
And carve me to shreds and cut me!" This
  now
Is your blessing, Mila di Codra!

MILA

It is just, it is just that you
Strike me thus! Just is it that you
Make my lips drink thus deep of this bitter-
    ness!
With such sorrow be accompanied
All these my sins to the world that's beyond!
Mayhap, mayhap, then, the stones and the
    heather
And the stubble, the woodblock dumb, un-
    feeling,
Shall speak for me, — the angel here silent,
That your brother is calling to life in the block
    there,
And the Virgin bereft of her lamplight.
These shall all speak for me: but I — I —
    shall speak not!

ORNELLA

Dear woman, indeed how around you
Your soul is your body's vestment,
And how I may touch it, outstretching
Towards you thus my hand with all faith.

123

How then did you do so much evil
To harm us so much — us — God's people?
If you could behold our Vienda,
Quiver, indeed, would you. For shortly the
    skin will
Over the bones part in twain for its dryness,
And the lips of her mouth are grown whiter
Than within her white mouth her white teeth
    are;
So that when the first rain came falling,
Saturday, Mamma, seeing her, said of her,
Weeping: "Lo, now! Lo, now! she will be
    leaving,
She will break with the moisture and vanish."
Yet my father laments not; his bitterness
He chews upon hard without weeping.
Envenomed within him the iron,
The wound in his flesh is like poison
(San Cresidio and San Rocca guard us!)
The swelling leaves only the mouth free
To bark at us daily and nightly.
In his frenzy his curses were fearful, —
The roof of the house with them shaking,

And with them our hearts quaking. Dear
    woman,
Your teeth are chattering. Have you the
    fever,
That you shiver thus and you tremble?

MILA

Always at twilight and sunset,
A tremor of cold overtakes me
Not strong am I in the nights on the mountain,
We light fires at this time in the valley,
But speak on and heed not my suffering.

ORNELLA

Yesterday, by chance, I discovered
He had it in mind to climb up here, —
This mountain to climb, to the sheepstead.
I failed through the evening to see him,
And my blood turned cold within me.
So then I made ready this basket,
And in this my sisters aided me, —
We are three who are born of one mother, —
All three of us born marked with sorrow;

And this morning I left Acquanova,
I crossed by the ferry the river,
And the path to the mountain ascended.
Ah! you dear, dear creature of Jesus!
With what illness now are you taken?
How can I bear all this sorrow?
What can I be doing for you?
You far more violently tremble
Than when you sought our fireplace
And the pack of the reapers were hunting you.

MILA

And since — Oh! since have you seen him?
    Know you
If yet he has come to the sheepstead?
Be certain, Ornella, be certain!

ORNELLA

Not again have I seen him. Nor yet
Do I know if he came up the mountain, —
Since much did he have for the doing
At Gionco. Perhaps he came not.
So do not be frightened! But hear me,

126

And heed me. For your soul's sake,
To save it, now, Mila di Codra,
Repent ye and take ye, I prithee,
Away from us this evil doing!
Restore us Aligi, and may God go with you,
And may He have mercy upon you!

MILA

Dear sister of Aligi! Content am I, —
Yea, always to hear and to heed you.
Just is it that you strike me, —
Me, the sinful woman, me, the sorcerer's
Daughter, the witch who is shameless, —
Who for charity supplicated
The journeying pilgrim of Jesus
But a little oil to give her
To feed her sacred lamp-flame!
Perhaps behind me the Angel is weeping
Again as before; and the stones perhaps
Will speak for me, but I — shall speak not —
Shall speak not. But this say I only
In the name of sister, and if I say not
In truth, may my mother arise

From her grave, my hair grasping,
And cast me upon the black earth, bearing
Witness against her own daughter.
Only say I: I am sinless before your brother,
Before the pallet of your brother clean am I!

ORNELLA

Omnipotent God! A miracle dost Thou!

MILA

But this is the loving of Mila.
This is but my love, Ornella.
And more than this I shall speak not.
Contented am I to obey you.
All paths knows the daughter of Jorio,
Already her soul ere your coming
Had started, — ere now, O Innocent One!
Do not distrust me, O sister
Of Aligi, for no cause is there.

ORNELLA

Firm as the rock my faith is in you.
Brow unto brow have I seen in you

128

Truth. And the rest lies in darkness,
That I, poor one, may not fathom.
But I kiss your feet here humbly,
The feet that know well the pathways.
And my silent love and pity
Will companion you on your journey.
I will pray that the steps of your pathway
Be lessened, the pain of them softened.
And the pain that I feel and I suffer
On your head I shall lay it no longer.
No more shall I judge your misfortunes,
No more shall I judge of your loving,
Since before my dear brother sinless
Are you, in my heart I shall call you
My sister, my sister in exile. At dawning
My dreams shall meet you and often shall
   greet you.

MILA

Ah, in my grave were I resting,
With the black earth close to me nestling,
And in my ears, in that grave lonely,
These words were the last words sounding, —
Their promise of peace my life rounding!

129

ORNELLA

For your life I have spoken, I witness.
And food and drink to restore you, —
That at least for the first of your journey,
You may not lack something of comfort, —
For you I prepared in this basket;
Bread placing in it and wine (the oil is now
Gone!) but I did not place there a flower.
Forgive me for that, since then I knew not —

MILA

A blue flower, a flower of the blue aconite —
You did not place that in your baskct for me!
And you did not place there the white sheet
    severed
From the cloth in your loom at home woven
That I saw 'twixt the doorway and fireplace!

ORNELLA

Mila! for that hour wait on the Saviour.
But what still keeps my brother? Vainly
I sought him at the sheepfold. Oh! where
    is he?

MILA

He will be back again ere nightfall surely.
Needs be that I hasten! O, needs be!

ORNELLA

Do you mean not to see him — speak again
    to him?
Where then will you go for this night? Re-
    main here.
I, too, will remain. Thus doing shall we
Be together, and strong against sorrow,
We three — Till you go at daybreak
On your path, and we go upon our path.

MILA

But already too long are the nights. Needs be
That I hasten, — hasten! You know not.
I will tell you. Also from him I received
The parting that's not to be given
A second time. Addio! Go, seek him,
And meet him, now, in the sheepfold, surely.
Detain him there longer, and tell him
All the grief that they suffer down there,

And let him not follow me! On my path-
way
Unknown, I shall soon be. Rest you blessèd!
Forever rest blessèd! O, be you as sweet
Unto his as you were to my sorrow!
Addio! Ornella, Ornella, Ornella!

[*While speaking thus, she retires toward
the darkness of the cavern and* ORNELLA,
*softened to tears, passes out. The old herb-
woman then appears at the opening of the
cavern. The singing of the pilgrims may still
be heard, but from a greater distance.* ANNA
ONNA *enters, leaning on her crutch with her
bag hanging by her side.*]

ANNA [*breathless*]

'Has freed him, freed him, woman of the valley,
'Has freed him! Ay! from inside him
Chased away all the demons did he —
Cosma — that possessed him. A saint, surely.
He gave out a great cry like a bull's roar, —
Did the youth, and at one blow fell down
As if he had burst his chest open.

132

You did n't — don't say you could n't — hear
    him?
And now on the grass he is sleeping.
Deeply, deeply is he sleeping; and the shep-
    herds
Stand around and keep watch o'er him.
But where are you? I do not see you.

MILA

Anna Onna, put me to sleep!
O Granny dear, I 'll give you this basket
That is brimful of eating and drinking.

ANNA

Who was she that went away hurrying?
Had she broken your heart that you cried so?
— That after her, so, you were calling?

MILA

Granny, oh, listen! This basket I 'll give you,
That one on the ground, to take with you, —
If you 'll put me to sleep, — make me go, —

To sleep, with the little black seeds — you
   know —
Of the hyoscyamus. Go off then! be eating
   and drinking!

ANNA

I have none. I have none left in my bag here!

MILA

The skin I will give you, too, the sheepskin
You were sleeping on here to-day.
If you give me some of those red seed-pods,
The red pods you know — twigs of the nasso.
Go off, then, go off, and fill up and guzzle!

ANNA

I have none, I have none in my bag here.
Go slower a bit, woman of the valley,
Take time, go slowly, go slowly,
Think it over a day, or a month, or a year.

MILA

O Granny dear, more will I give you!
A kerchief with pictures in color,

134

And of woollen cloth, three arms' lengths,
If you give me some of the herb-roots —
The same that you sell to the shepherds
That kill off the wolves so swiftly —
The root of the wolf-grass, the wolf-bane —
Go off then. Go off and mend up your bones!

ANNA

I have none, I have none left in my bag
    here.
Go slower a bit, woman of the valley,
Take time, go slowly, go slowly,
With time there always comes wisdom.
Think it over a day, or a month, or a year,
With the herbs of the good Mother Mountain
We can heal all our ailments and sorrows.

MILA

You will not? Very well then, I snatch thus
    from you
That black bag of yours. Therein I 'll be
    finding
What will serve for me well, well indeed!

135

[*She tries to tear the bag away from the tottering old woman.*]

ANNA

No, no. You are robbing me, your poor old
  granny,
You force me! The shepherd — he 'd tear
  me —
Gouge out my eyes from their sockets.

[*A step is heard and a man's form appears in the shadows.*]

MILA

Ah! it is you, it is you, Aligi!
Behold what this woman is doing.

[MILA *lets fall the bag which she had taken from the old woman and sees the man looming tall in the dim light of the mountain, but recognizing him she takes refuge in the depths of the cavern.* LAZARO DI ROIO *then enters, silent, with a rope around his arm like an ox drover about to tie up his beast. The sound of* ANNA ONNA's *crutches striking against the stones is heard as she departs in safety.*]

LAZARO

Woman, O, you need not be frightened.
Lazaro di Roio has come here,
But he does not carry his sickle:
It is scarcely a case of an eye for an eye,
And he does not wish to enforce it.
There was more than an ounce of blood taken
From him on the wheat-field of Mispa,
And you know cause and end of that bloodshed.
Ounce for ounce, then, he will not take from
    you,
Nor wish it, for all the wound's smarting —
The cicatrice, here in the forehead.
Raven feather, olive-twig crook,
Rancid oil, soot from the chimney shook,
Morn unto eve, eve unto morn,
The cursèd wound must healing scorn!

[*He gives a short, malignant laugh.*]

And where I was lying, I heard ever
The weeping and wailing, the women,
Oh, not for me, but this shepherd,
Spell-bound, bewitched by the witch shrew

137

Way off in the far-away mountain.
Surely, woman, poor was your picking.
But my grit and my blood are back again,
And many words I shall not be talking,
My tongue is dry now for doing it,
And all for this same sad occasion.
Now then, say I, you shall come on with me,
And no talk about it, daughter of Jorio!
Waiting below is the donkey and saddle,
And also here a good rope hempen,
And others to spare, God be praised! if need
    be!

[MILA *remains motionless, backed up
against the rock, without replying.*]

Did you hear me, Mila di Codra?
Or are you deaf and dumb now?
This I am saying in quiet:
I know all about how it happened,
That time with the reapers of Norca.
If you are thinking to thwart me
With the same old tricks, undeceive you!
There 's no fireplace here, nor any

Relations, nor San Giovanni
Ringing the bells of salvation.
I take three steps and I seize you,
With two good stout fellows to help me.
So now, then, and I say it in quiet,
You 'd better agree to what needs be.
You may just as well do as I want you,
For if you don't do so, you 'll have to!

MILA

What do you want from me? Where already
Death was, you came. Death is here, even
   now.
He stepped one side to let you enter.
Withdrawing awhile, still here he is waiting.
Oh, pick up that bag there; inside it
Are deadly roots enough to kill ten wolves.
If you bind it on to my jaws here
I would make of it all a good mouthful;
I would eat therein, you would see me,
As the good hungry mare that crunches
Her oats. So then, when I should be
Cold, you could take me up there and toss me

And pack me upon your donkey,
And tie with your rope like a bundle,
And shout out: " Behold the witch, shameless,
The sorceress!" Let them burn up my body,
Let the women come round and behold me,
And rejoice in deliverance. Mayhap
One would thrust in her hand, in the fire,
Without being burned in the flame,
And draw from the core of the heat my heart.

[LAZARO, *at her first bidding, takes up the*
bag and examines the simples. He then throws
it behind him, with suspicion and distrust.]

LAZARO

Ah, ah! You want to spread some snare.
What crouch are you watching to spring on
    me!
In your voice I can hear all your slyness,
But I shall trap you in my lariat.

[*At this he makes his rope into a lariat.*]

Not dead, neither cold do I want you.
Lazaro di Roio, — by all the gods! —

Mila di Codra, will harvest you, —
Will go with you this very October,
And for this all things are ready.
He will press the grapes with your body,
Lazaro will sink in the must with you.

[*With a sinister laugh he advances toward*
MILA, *who is on the alert to elude him, the man
following closely, she darting here and there,
unable to escape him.*]

MILA

Do not touch me! Be ashamed of yourself!
For your own son is standing behind you.

[ALIGI *appears at the end of the cave.
Seeing his father, he turns pale.* LAZARO, *halting in his chase, turns toward him. Father and
son regard each other intently and ominously.*]

LAZARO

Hola there, Aligi! What is it?

ALIGI

Father, how did you come hither?

141

LAZARO

Has your blood been all sucked up that it's
    made you
So pale? As white you stand there in the light
As the whey when they squeeze out the cheeses.
Shepherd, say, why are you frightened?

ALIGI

Father, what is it you wish to do here?

LAZARO

What I wish to do here? You are asking
A question of me, a right you have not.
I will tell you, however. This will I:
The yearling ewe catch in my lariat,
And lead her wherever it please me.
That done, I shall sentence the shepherd.

ALIGI

Father, this thing you shall surely not do.

LAZARO

How dare you then lift so boldly
Your white face up into mine? Be careful

142

Or I shall make it blush of a sudden.
Go! turn back to your sheepfold and stay
　　there,
With your flock inside the enclosure,
Until I come there to seek you.
On your life, I say, obey me!

ALIGI

Father, I pray the Saviour to keep me
From doing you aught but obedience.
And you are able to judge and to sentence
This son of your own; but this one —
This woman, see that you leave her alone!
Leave her to weep here alone.
Do no offence unto her.   It is sinful.

LAZARO

Ah!   The Lord has made you crazy!
Of what saint were you just speaking?
See you not (may your eyes be blind forever!)
See you not how under her eyelashes, —
Around her neck lie hidden
The seven sins, the mortal sins?

Surely, if there should see her only
Your buck now, 't would butt her, and you here
Are frightened lest I should offend her!
I tell you the stones of the highroad
By man and by beast are less trodden
Than she is by sin and shame trampled.

ALIGI

If it were not a sin unto God in me,
If by all men it were not deemed evil,
Father, I should say unto you that in this
    thing, —
In this thing you lie in your gullet!

[*He takes a few steps and places himself
between his father and the woman, covering
her with his body.*]

LAZARO

What 's that you say? Your tongue in you
    wither!
Down on your knees there, to beg me
Forgiveness, your face on the ground there!
And never dare you to lift up your body

144

Before me! Thus, on your marrow-bones,
Off with you! Herd with your dogs!

ALIGI

The Saviour will judge of me, father:
But this woman I shall not abandon,
Nor unto your wrath shall I leave her,
While living. The Saviour will judge me.

LAZARO

I am the judge of you. Who
Am I then to you, blood and body?

ALIGI

You are my own father, dear unto me.

LAZARO

I am unto you your own father, and to you
I may do as to me it seem pleasing
Because unto me you are but the ox
In my stable; you are but my shovel
And hoe. And if I should over you
Pass with my harrow and tear you

145

And break you in pieces, this is well done!
And if I have need of a handle
For my knife, and one I shall make myself
Out of one of your bones, this is well done!
Because I am the father and you are the son!
Do you heed? And to me over you is given
All power, since time beyond time,
And a law that is over all laws.
And as even I was to my father,
So even are you unto me, under earth.
Do you heed? And if from your memory
This thing has fallen, then thus I recall
It unto your memory. Kneel down on your
　　knees and kiss ye
The earth on your marrow-bones
And go off without looking behind you!

ALIGI

Pass over me then with the harrow;
But touch not the woman.

[LAZARO *goes up to him, unable to restrain
his rage, and lifting the rope, strikes him on the
shoulder.*]

LAZARO

Down, down, you dog, down, to the ground
with you!

ALIGI [*falling on his knees*]

So then, my father, I kneel down before you:
The ground in front of you do I kiss,
And in the name of the true God and living
By my first tear and my infant wailing
From the time when you took me unswaddled
And in your hand held me aloft
Before the sacred face of Lord Christ, —
By all this, I beseech you, I pray you, my
    father,
That you tread not thus and trample
On the heart of your son sorrow-laden.
Do not thus disgrace him! I pray you:
Do not make his senses forsake him,
Nor deliver him into the hands of the False
    One —
The Enemy who wheels now about us!
I pray you by the angel there silent,
Who sees and who hears in that wood block!

147

LAZARO

Begone! Off with you! Off with you!
I shall shortly now judge of you.
Off with you, I bid you. Be off with you!

[*He strikes him cruelly with the rope.*
Aligi *rises all quivering.*]

ALIGI

Let the Saviour be judge. Let him judge then
Between you and me, and let him give unto me
Light; but yet I will against you
Not lift up this my hand.

LAZARO

Be you damned! With this rope I will hang
you.

[*He throws the lariat to take him but*
Aligi, *seizing the rope with a sudden jerk,
takes it out of his father's hands.*]

ALIGI

Christ my Saviour, help Thou me!
That I may not uplift my hand against him,
That I may not do this to my father!

148

LAZARO [*furious, goes to the door and calls*]

Ho, Jenne! and ho, Femo! Come here!
Come here, and see this fellow,
What he is doing (may a viper sting him!)
Fetch the ropes. Possessed is he
Most surely. His own father he threatens!

[*Running appear two men, big and muscular, bearing ropes.*]

He is rebellious, this fellow!
From the womb is he damned,
And for all his days and beyond them.
The evil spirit has entered into him.
See! See! Behold how bloodless
The face is. O Jenne! You take him and
    hold him.
O Femo, you have the rope, take it and bind
    him,
For to stain myself I am not wishing.
Then go ye and seek out some one
To perform the exconjuration.

[*The two men throw themselves upon* ALIGI
and overpower him.]

149

ALIGI

Brothers in God! O, do not do this to me!
Do not imperil your soul, Jenne.
I who know you so well, who remember,
Remember you well from a baby,
Since you came as a boy to pick up the olives
In your fields. O Jenne dell Eta!
I remember you. Do not thus debase me.
Do not thus disgrace me!

[*They hold him tightly, trying to bind him,
and pushing him on toward the entrance.*]

Ah! dog! — The pest take you! —
No, no, no! — Mila, Mila! Hasten! —
Give me the iron there. Mila! Mila!

[*His voice, desperate and hoarse, is heard
in the distance, while* LAZARO *bars* MILA's
egress.]

MILA

Aligi, Aligi! Heaven help you!
May God avenge you! Never despair!
No power have I, no power have you,

But while I have breath in my mouth,
I am all yours! I am all for you!
Have faith! Have faith! Help shall come!
Be of good heart, Aligi! May God help you!

[Mila *gazes intently along the path where
*Aligi *was borne and listens intently for voices.
In this brief interval *Lazaro *scrutinizes the
cavern insidiously. From the distance comes
the singing of another company of pilgrims
crossing the valley.*]

LAZARO

Woman, now then you have been seeing
How I am the man here. I give out the law.
You are left here alone with me.
Night is approaching, and inside here
It is now almost night. O don't
Be afraid of me, Mila di Codra,
Nor yet of this red scar of mine
If you see it light up, for now even
I feel in it the beat of the fever.
Come nearer me. Quite worn out you seem
    to be

For sure you 've not met with fat living
On this hard shepherd's pallet.
While with me you shall have, if you want it,
All of that in the valley; for Lazaro
Di Roio is one of the thrifty.
But what do you spy at? Whom do you wait
for?

MILA

No one I wait for. No one is coming!

[*She is still motionless, hoping to see*
ORNELLA *come and save her. Dissimulating
to gain time, she tries to defeat* LAZARO's
intentions.]

LAZARO

You are alone with me. You need not
Be frightened. Are you persuaded?

MILA [*hesitatingly*]

I 'm thinking, Lazaro di Roio.
I 'm thinking of what you have promised.
I 'm thinking. But what 's to secure me?

152

LAZARO

Do not draw back. My word I keep.
All that I promise, I tell you.
Be assured, God be witness. Come to me!

MILA

And Candia della Leonessa?

LAZARO

Let the bitterness of her mouth moisten
Her thread, and with that be her weaving!

MILA

—The three daughters you have in your house-
    hold?
And now the new one! — I dare not trust to it.

LAZARO

Come here! Don't draw back! Here! Feel it!
Where I tucked it. Twenty ducats,
Sewed in this coat. Do you want them?

[*He feels for them through his goatskin
coat, then takes it off and throws it on the
ground at her feet.*]

153

Take them! Don't you hear them clinking?
There are twenty silver ducats.

MILA

But first I must see them and count them, —
First — before — Lazaro di Roio.
Now will I take these shears and rip it.

LAZARO

But why spy about so? You witch! surely
You 're getting some little trick ready.
You 're hoping yet you 'll deceive me.

[*He makes a rush at her to seize her. She
eludes him and seeks refuge near the walnut
block.*]

MILA

No, no, no! Let me alone! Let me alone!
Don't you touch me! See! See! She comes!
  See! See! she comes

Your own daughter — Ornella is coming.

[*She grasps the angel to resist* LAZARO's
violence.]

No, no! Ornella, Ornella, O help me!

THE PARRICIDE.

Act II., Page 155.

[*Suddenly* ALIGI *appears, free and un-bound, at the mouth of the cave. He sees in the dim light the two figures. He throws him-self upon his father. Catching sight of the axe driven into the wood, he seizes it, blind with fury and horror.*]

ALIGI

Let her go! For your life!

[*He strikes his father to death.* ORNELLA, *just appearing, bends down and recognizes the dead body in the shadow of the angel. She utters a great cry.*]

ORNELLA

Ah! I untied him! I untied him!

ACT III.

A LARGE *country yard; in the farther end an oak, venerable with age, beyond the fields, bounded by mountains, furrowed by torrents; on the left the house of* LAZARO, *the door open, the porch littered with agricultural implements; on the right the haystack, the mill, and the straw stack.*

The body of LAZARO *is lying on the floor within the house, the head resting, according to custom for one murdered, on a bundle of grape-vine twigs; the wailers, kneeling, surround the body, one of them intoning the lamentation, the others answering. At times they bow toward one another, bending till they bring their foreheads together. On the porch, between the plough and large earthen vessel, are the kindred and* SPLENDORE *and* FAVETTA. *Farther from them is* VIENDA DI GIAVE, *sitting*

on a hewn stone, looking pale and desolate,
with the look of one dying, her mother and god-
mother consoling her. ORNELLA *is under the*
tree, alone, her head turned toward the path.
All are in mourning.

CHORUS OF WAILERS

Jesu, Saviour, Jesu, Saviour!
'T is your will. 'T is your bidding,
That a tragic death accursèd
Lazaro fell by and perished.
From peak unto peak ran the shudder,
All of the mountain was shaken.
Veiled was the sun in heaven,
Hidden his face was and covered.
Woe! Woe! Lazaro, Lazaro, Lazaro!
Alas! What tears for thee tear us!
Requiem æternam dona ei, Domine.
(O Lord! give him rest eternal.)

ORNELLA

Now, now! Coming! 'T is coming! Far off!
The black standard! The dust rising!

157

O sisters, my sisters, think, oh! think
Of the mother, how to prepare her! —
That her heart may not break. But a little
And he will be here. Lo! at the near turn,
At the near turn the standard appearing!

SPLENDORE

Mother of the passion of the Son crucified,
You and you only can tell the mother, —
Go to the mother, to her heart whisper!

[*Some of the women go out to see.*]

ANNA DI BOVE

It is the cypress of the field of Fiamorbo.

FELAVIA SESARA

It is the shadow of clouds passing over.

ORNELLA

It is neither the cypress nor shadow
Of storm-cloud, dear women, I see it advancing,

Neither cypress nor storm-cloud, woe's me!
But the Standard and Sign of Wrong-Doing
That is borne along with him. He's coming
The condemned one's farewells to receive here,
To take from the hands of the mother
The cup of forgetting, ere to God he commend
    him.
Ah! wherefore are we not all of us dying,
Dying with him? My sisters, my sisters!

[*The sisters all look out the gate toward the path.*]

THE CHORUS OF WAILERS

Jesu, Jesu, it were better
That this roof should on us crumble.
Ah! Too much is this great sorrow,
Candia della Leonessa.
On the bare ground your husband lying,
Not even permitted a pillow,
But only a bundle of vine-twigs,
Under his head where he's lying.
Woe! woe! Lazaro, Lazaro, Lazaro!
Alas! What pain for thee pains us!
Requiem æternam dona ei, Domine.

159

SPLENDORE

Favetta, go you; go speak to her.
Go you, touch her on the shoulder.
So she may feel and turn. She is seated
Like unto a stone on the hearthstone,
Stays fixed there without moving an eyelash,
And she seems to see nothing, hear nothing;
She seems to be one with the hearthstone.
Dear Virgin of mercy and pity!
Her senses O do not take from her! — Un-
    happy one!
Cause her to heed us, and in our eyes
    looking
To come to herself, dear unhappy one.
Yet I have no heart even to touch her,
And who then will say the word to her?
O sister! Go tell her: Lo! he is coming!

FAVETTA

Nor have I the heart. She affrights me.
How she looked before I seem to forget,
And how her voice sounded before,
Ere in the deep of this sorrow

160

We plunged. Her head has whitened
And it grows every hour whiter.
Oh! she is scarcely ours any more,
She seems from us so far away,
As if on that stone she were seated
For years a hundred times one hundred —
From one hundred years to another —
And had lost, quite lost remembrance
Of us. — O just see now, just see now,
Her mouth, how shut her mouth is!
More shut than the mouth that's made
    silent, —
Mute on the ground there forever.
How then can she speak to us ever?
I will not touch her nor can I tell her —
" Lo! he is coming! " If she awaken
She 'll fall, she 'll crumble. She affrights me!

SPLENDORE

O wherefore were we born, my sisters?
And wherefore brought forth by our mother?
Let us all in one sheaf be gathered,
And let Death bear us all thus away!

161

THE CHORUS OF WAILERS

— Ah! mercy, mercy on you, Woman!
— Ah! mercy be upon you, Women!
— Up and take heart again! The Lord God
Will uplift whom he uprooted.
If God willed it that sad be the vintage
Mayhap He wills, too, that the olives
Be sure. Put your trust in the Lord.
— And sadder than you is another,
She who sat in her home well contented,
In plenty, mid bread and clean flour,
Entering here, fell asleep, to awaken
Amid foul misfortune and never
Again to smile. She is dying: Vienda.
Of the world beyond is she already.
— She is there without wailing or weeping!
Ah! on all human flesh have thou pity!
On all that are living have mercy!
And all who are born to suffer,
To suffer and know not wherefore!

ORNELLA

Oh, there Femo di Nerfa is coming,
The ox driver, hurriedly coming.

And there is the standard stopping
Beside the White Tabernacle.
My sisters, shall I myself go to her
And bear her the word?
Woe! oh, woe! If she does not remember
What is required of her. Lord God
Forbid that she be not ready
And all unprepared he come on her and call
    her,
For if his voice strike her ear on a sudden
Then surely her heart will be broken, broken!

ANNA DI BOVE

Then surely her heart will be broken,
Ornella, if you should go touch her,
For you bring bad fortune with you.
'T was you who barred up the doorway,
'T was you who unfettered Aligi.

THE CHORUS OF WAILERS

To whom are you leaving your ploughshare,
O Lazaro! to whom do you leave it?
Who now your fields will be tilling?

Who now your flocks will be leading?
Both father and son the Enemy
Has snared in his toils and taken.
Death of infamy! Death of infamy!
The rope, and the sack, and the blade of iron!
Woe! woe! Lazaro, Lazaro, Lazaro!
Alas! What torments for thee torment us!
Requiem æternam dona ei, Domine.

[*The ox driver appears, panting.*]

FEMO DI NERFA

Where is Candia? O ye daughters of the
    dead one!
Judgment is pronounced. Now kiss ye
The dust! Now grasp in your hands the ashes!
For now the Judge of Wrong-Doing
Has given the final sentence.
And all the People is the Executor
Of the Parricide, and in its hands it has him.
Now the People are bringing here your brother
That he may receive forgiveness
From his own mother, from his mother
Receive the cup of forgetfulness,

164

Before his right hand they shall sever,
Before in the leathern sack they sew him
With the savage mastiff and throw him
Where the deep restless waters o'erflow him!
All ye daughters of the dead one, kiss ye
The dust now; grasp in your hands now the
  ashes!
And may our Saviour, the Lord Jesus
Upon innocent blood have pity!

[*The three sisters rush up to each other,
and then advancing slowly, remain with their
heads touching each other. From the distance
is heard the sound of the muffled drum.*]

MARIA CORA

O Femo, how could you ever say it?

FEMO DI NERFA

Where is Candia? Why does she not appear
  here?

LA CINERELLA

On the hearthstone, the stone by the fireplace
She sits and gives no sign of living.

ANNA DI BOVA

And there's no one so hardy to touch her.

LA CINERELLA

And affrighted for her are her daughters.

FELAVIA SESARA

And you, Femo, did you bear witness?

LA CATALANA

And Aligi, did you have him near you?
And before the judge what did he utter?

MONICA DELLA COGNA

What said he? What did he? Aloud
Did he cry? Did he rave, the poor unfortu-
nate one?

FEMO DI NERFA

He fell on his knees and remained so,
And upon his own hand stayed gazing,
And at times he would say "*Mea culpa*,"
And would kiss the earth before him,

166

And his face looked sweet and humble,
As the face of one who was innocent.
And the angel carved out of the walnut block
Was near him there with the blood-stain.
And many about him were weeping,
And some of them said, " He is innocent."

ANNA DI BOVA

And that woman of darkness, Mila
Di Codra, has anyone seen her?

LA CATALANA

Where is the daughter of Jorio?
Was she not to be seen? What know you?

FEMO DI NERFA

They have searched all the sheepfolds and
    stables
Without any trace of her finding.
The shepherds have nowhere seen her,
Only Cosma, the saint of the mountain,
Seems to have seen her, and he says

167

That in some mountain gorge she 's gone to
cast her bones away.

LA CATALANA

May the crows find her yet living
And pick out her eyes. May the wolf-pack
Scent her yet living and tear her!

FELAVIA SESARA

And ever reborn to that torture
Be the damnable flesh of that woman!

MARIA CORA

Be still, be still, Felavia, silence, I say!
Be silent now! For Candia has arisen,
She is walking, coming to the threshold.
Now she goes out. O daughters, ye daughters,
She has arisen, support her!

[*The sisters separate and go toward the
door.*]

THE CHORUS OF WAILERS

Candia della Leonessa,
Whither go you? Who has called you?

168

Sealed up are your lips and silent,
And your feet are like feet fettered.
Death you are leaving behind you,
And sin you find coming to meet you.
Wheresoever going, wheresoever turning,
Thorny everywhere the pathway.
Oh! woe! woe! ashes, ashes, widow!
Oh! woe! mother, Jesu! Jesu! mercy!
De profundis clamavi ad te, Domine.
(Out of the deep, O Lord, I cry unto Thee!)

[*The mother appears at the threshold.
The daughters timidly go to support her. She
gazes at them in great bewilderment.*]

SPLENDORE

Mother, dearest, you have risen, maybe
You need something — refreshment —
A mouthful of muscadel, a cordial?

FAVETTA

Parched are your lips, you dear one,
And bleeding are they? Shall we not bathe
    them?

169

ORNELLA

Mommy, have courage, we are with you.
Unto this great trial God has called you.

CANDIA

And from one warp came so much linen,
And from one spring so many rivers,
And from one oak so many branches,
And from one mother many daughters!

ORNELLA

Mother dear, your forehead is fevered. For
   the weather
To-day is stifling, and your dress is heavy,
And your dear face is all wet with moisture.

MARIA CORA

Jesu, Jesu, may she not lose her senses!

LA CINERELLA

Help her regain her mind, Madonna!

CANDIA

It is so long since I did any singing,
I fear I cannot hold the melody.

170

But to-day is Friday, there is no singing,
Our Saviour went to the mountain this day.

SPLENDORE

O mother dear, where does your mind wander?
Look at us! Know us! What idle fancy
Teases you? Wretched are we! What is her
    meaning?

CANDIA

Here, too, is the stole, and here, too, is the
    cup sacramental,
And this is the belfry of San Biagio.
And this is the river, and this my own cabin.
But who, who is this one who stands in my
    doorway?

[*Sudden terror seizes the young girls.
They draw back, watching their mother, moan-
ing and weeping.*]

ORNELLA

O my sisters, we have lost her!
Lost her, also, our dear mother!
Oh! too far away do her senses stray!

171

SPLENDORE

Unhappy we! Whom God's malediction left
Alone in the land, orphans bereft!

FAVETTA

By the other, a new grave make ready near
And bury us living all unready here!

FELAVIA SESARA

No no, dear girls, be not so despairing,
For the shock is but pushing her senses
Far back to some time long ago.
Let them wander! thence soon to be turning!

[CANDIA *takes several steps.*]

ORNELLA

Mother, you hear me? Where are you going?

CANDIA

I have lost the heart of my dear gentle boy,
Thirty-three days ago now, nor yet do I
    find it;

172

Have you seen him anywhere? Have you
    met him afar?
— Upon Calvary Mountain I left him,
I left him afar on the distant mountain,
I left him afar in tears and bleeding.

MARIA CORA

Ah! she is telling her stations.

FELAVIA SESARA

Let her mind wander, let her say them!

LA CINERELLA

Let her all her heart unburden!

MONICA DELLA COGNA

O Madonna of Holy Friday,
Have pity on her! And pray for us!
        [*The two women kneel and pray.*]

CANDIA

Lo! now the mother sets out on her travels,
To visit her son well belovèd she travels.

— O Mother, Mother, wherefore your com-
ing?
Among these Judeans there is no safety.
— An armful of linen cloth I am bringing
To swathe the sore wounds of your body.
— Ah! me! had you brought but a swallow
of water!
— My son! — No pathway I know nor well-
spring;
But if you will bend your dear head a little
A throatful of milk from my breast I will
give you,
And if then you find there no milk, oh so
closely
To heart I will press you, my life will go to
you!
— O Mother, Mother, speak softly, softly —

[*She stops for a moment, then dragging
her words, cries out suddenly with a despairing
cry.*]

Mother, I have been sleeping for years seven
hundred,

Years seven hundred, I come from afar off.
I no longer remember the days of my cradle.

[*Struck by her own voice she stops and
looks about bewildered, as if suddenly awakened from a dream. Her daughters hasten
to support her. The women all rise. The
beating of the drum sounds less muffled, as
if approaching.*]

ORNELLA

Ah! how she 's trembling, how she 's all trem-
    bling!
Now she swoons. Her heart is almost broken.
For two days she has tasted nothing. Gone
    is she!

SPLENDORE

Mamma, who is it speaks within you? What
    do you feel,
Speaking inside you, in the breast of you?

FAVETTA

Oh! unto us hearken; heed us, mother,
Oh! look upon us! We are here with you!

175

FEMO DI NERFA [*from the end of the yard*]

O women, women, he 's near, the crowd with
him.
The standard is passing the cistern now.
They are bringing also the angel covered.

[*The women gather under the oak to
watch.*]

ORNELLA [*in a loud voice*]

Mother, Aligi is coming now; Aligi is
coming,
To take from your heart the token of pardon,
And drink from your hand the cup of forget-
fulness.
Awaken, awaken, be brave, dear mother;
Accursèd he is not. With deep repentance
The sacred blood he has spilled redeeming.

CANDIA

'T is true; oh, 't is true. With the leaves he
was bruising
They stanched the blood that was gushing.
" Son Aligi," he said then, " Son Aligi,

176

Let go the sickle and take up the sheep-
     crook,
Be you the shepherd and go to the mountain."
This his commandment was kept in obedience.

SPLENDORE

Do you well understand? Aligi is coming.

CANDIA

And unto the mountain he must be returning.
What shall I do? All his new clothing
I have not yet made ready, Ornella!

ORNELLA

Mother, let us take this step. Turn now unto
     us; here,
In front of the house we must await him
And give our farewell to him who is leaving,
Then all in peace we shall lie down together,
Side by side in the deep bed below.

     [*The daughters lead their mother out on
the porch.*]

177

CANDIA [*murmuring to herself*]

I lay down and meseemed of Jesus I dreamed,
He came to me saying, " Be not fearful! "
San Giovanni said to me, " Rest in safety."

THE CHORUS OF KINDRED

— Oh what crowds of people follow the stand-
    ard,
The whole village is coming after.
— Iona di Midia is carrying the standard.
— Oh how still it is, like a processional!
— Oh what sadness! On his head the veil of
    sable,
— On his hands the wooden fetters,
Large and heavy, big as an ox-yoke!
Head to foot the gray cloth wraps him, he is
    barefoot.
— Ah! Who can look longer! My face I
    bury,
I close up my eyes from longer seeing.
— The leathern sack Leonardo is bearing,
Biagio Gudo leads the savage mastiff.
— Mix in with the wine the roots of solatro

That he may lose his consciousness.

— Brew with the wine the herb novella

That he may lose feeling, miss suffering.

Go, Maria Cora, you who know the secrets,

Help Ornella to mix the potion.

— Dire was the deed, dire is the suffering.

Oh what sadness! See the people!

— Silently comes all the village.

— Abandoned now are all the vineyards.

— To-day, to-day no grapes are gathered.

— Yes, to-day even the land is mourning.

— Who is not weeping? Who is not wailing?

— See Vienda! Almost in death's agony.

Better for her that she lost her senses.

— Better for her that she see not, hear not.

— O woe for her bitter fate, three months only

Since we came and brought our hampers!

— And sorrow yet to come who may measure?

— No tears shall be left in us for weeping.

FEMO DI NERFA

Silence, O kindred, for here comes Iona.

[*The women turn toward the porch. There is a deep silence. The voice of* IONA]

IONA

O widow of Lazaro di Roio,
O people of this unhappy home,
Behold now! Behold now! The penitent is
    coming.

[*The tall figure of* IONA *appears bearing the standard. Behind him comes the parricide, robed in gray, the head covered with a black veil, both hands manacled in heavy wooden fetters. A man on one side is holding the shepherd's carved crook; others carry the angel covered with a white cloth, which they lower to the ground. The crowd pushes between the straw stack and ancient oak. The wailers, still on their knees, crawl to the door and lift up their voices in cries and wailing towards the condemned one.*]

180

THE CHORUS OF WAILERS

Son, O son Aligi!   Son, O son Aligi!
What have you done?   What have you done?
Whose body is this body bleeding?
And who upon the stone has placed it?
Now hath come your hour upon you!
Black is the wine of the evil-doer!
Severed hand and death of infamy;
Severed hand and sack of leather!
Oh! woe! woe!   O son of Lazaro.   Lazaro
Is dead.   Woe!   Woe!   And you slew Lazaro!
Libera, Domine, animam servi tui.
(Spare, O Lord, the soul of this thy servant.)

IONA DI MIDIA

Grief is yours, Candia della Leonessa,
O Vienda di Giave, grief is yours,
Grief is yours, daughters of the dead one!
    Kindred,
May the Lord Saviour have pity on all of
    you, women,
For into the hands of the People, judging,
The Judge has now given Aligi di Lazaro.

181

That upon the deed infamous we may take
vengeance,
A deed upon all of us fallen, and having no
equal,
Nor among our ancestors known to memory,
And may it forever be lost from memory,
By the grace of the Lord, from son to son,
henceforth.
Now, therefore, the penitent one we lead
hither,
That he may receive the cup of forget-
fulness
From you here, Candia della Leonessa,
Since he out of your flesh and your blood was
the issue,
To you 't is conceded to lift the veil of sable,
'T is yielded you lift to his mouth the cup of
forgetting,
Since his death unto him shall be exceeding
bitter.
Salvum fac populum tuum, Domine!
(Save, O Lord, these thy people)
Kyrie eleison!

THE CROWD

Christe eleison, Kyrie eleison!

[Iona *places his hand on* Aligi's *shoulder. The penitent then takes a step toward his mother, and falls, as if broken down, upon his knees.*]

ALIGI

Praises to Jesus and to Mary!
I can call you no longer my mother,
'T is given to me to bless you no longer.
This is the mouth of hell — this mouth!
To curses only these lips are given,
That sucked from you the milk of life,
That from your lips learned orisons holy
In the fear of the Lord God Almighty,
And of all of his law and commandments.
Why have I brought upon you this evil? —
You — of all women born to nourish the child,
To sing him to sleep on the lap, in the
    cradle! —
This would I say of my will within me,
But locked must my lips remain.

— Oh, no! Lift not up my veil of darkness
Lest thus in its fold you behold
The face of my terrible sinning.
Do not lift up my veil of darkness,
No, nor give me the cup of forgetting.
Then but little shall be my suffering,
But little the suffering decreed me.
Rather chase me with stones away,
Ay, with stones and with staves drive and
　　chase me,
As you would chase off the mastiff even
Soon to be of my anguish companion,
And to tear at my throat and mumble it,
While my desperate spirit within me
Shall cry aloud, "Mamma! Mamma!"
When the stump of my arm is reeking
In the cursèd sack of infamy.

THE CROWD [*with hushed voices*]

— Ah! the mother, poor dear soul! See her!
See how in two nights she has whitened!
She does not weep. She can weep no longer.
— Bereft is she of her senses.

— Not moving at all.   Like the statue
Of our Mater Dolorosa.   O have pity!
— O good Lord, have mercy on her!
Blessed Virgin, pity, help her!
— Jesus Christ have pity on her!

ALIGI

And you also, my dear ones, no longer
'T is given me to call you sisters,
'T is given me no longer to name you
By your names in your baptisms christened.
Like leaves of mint your names unto me,
In my mouth like leaves that are fragrant,
That brought unto me in the pastures
Unto my heart joy and freshness.
And now on my lips do I feel them,
And aloud am I fain to say them.
I crave no other consolation
Than that for my spirit's passing.
But no longer to name them 't is given me.
And now the sweet names must faint and
    wither,
For who shall be lovers to sing them

185

At eve beneath your casement windows?
For who shall be lovers unto the sisters
Of Aligi? And now is the honey
Turned into bitterness; O then, chase me,
And, like a hound, hound me away.
With staves and with stones strike me.
But ere you thus chase me, O suffer
That I leave unto you, disconsolate,
But these two things of my sole possession,
The things that these kindly people
Carry for me: the sheep-crook of bloodwood,
Whereon I carved the three virgin sisters,
In your likeness did I carve them,
To wander the mountain pastures with me, —
The sheep-crook, and the silent angel,
That with my soul I have been carving.
Woe is me for the stain that stains it!
But the stain that stains it shall fade away
Some day, and the angel now silent
Shall speak some day, and you shall hearken,
And you shall heed. Suffer me suffer
For all I have done! With my woe profound
In comparison little I suffer!

186

THE CROWD

Oh! the children, poor dear souls! See them!
See how pale and how worn are their faces!
— They too are no longer weeping
— They have no tears left for weeping.
Dry their eyes are, inward burning.
— Death has mown them with his sickle, —
To the ground laid them low ere their dying.
Down they are mown but not gathered.
— Have mercy upon them, O merciful one!
Upon these thy creatures so innocent.
— Pity, Lord Jesus, pity! Pity!

ALIGI

And you who are maiden and widow,
Who have found in the chests of your bridal
Only the vestment of mourning,
The combs of ebon, of thorns the necklace,
Your fine linen woven of tribulation,
Full of weeping your days ever more,
In heaven shall you have your nuptials,
And may you be spouse unto Jesus!
And Mary console you forever!

187

THE CROWD

O poor dear one! Until vespers
Hardly lasting, and now drawing
Her last breath. Lost her face is
In her hair of gold all faded,
Even all her golden tresses.
— Now like flax upon the distaff,
— Or shade-grown grass for Holy Thursday.
— Yes, Vienda, maiden-widow,
Paradise is waiting for you.
— If she is not, then who is Heaven's?
— May Our Lady take you with her!
— Put her with the white pure angels!
— Put her with the golden martyrs!

IONA DI MIDIA

Aligi, your farewells are spoken,
Rise now and depart. It grows late.
Ere long will the sun be setting.
To the Ave Maria you shall not hearken.
The evening star you shall not see glimmer.
O Candia della Leonessa,
If you, poor soul, on him have pity,

Give, if you will, the cup, not delaying,
For the mother art thou, and may console him.

THE CROWD

Candia, lift up the veil, Candia!
Press his lips to the cup, Candia,
Give him the potion, give him
Heart to bear his suffering. Rise, Candia!
— Upon your own son take pity.
— You only can help him; to you, 't is granted.
— Have mercy upon him! Mercy, O mercy!

[ORNELLA *hands the mother the cup containing the potion.* FAVETTA *and* SPLENDORE *encourage the poor mother.* ALIGI, *kneeling, creeps to the door of the house and addresses the dead body.*]

ALIGI

Father, father, my father Lazaro,
Hear me. You have crossed over the river,
In your bier, though it was heavier
Than the ox-cart, your bier was,
And the rock was dropped in the river.
Where the current was swiftest, you crossed it;

189

Father, father, my father Lazaro,
Hear me. Now I also would cross over
The river, but I — I cannot. I am going
To seek out that rock at the bottom.
And then I shall go to find you:
And over me you will pass the harrow,
Through all eternity to tear me,
Through all eternity to lacerate me.
Father of mine, full soon I 'll be with you!

[*The mother goes toward him in deep horror. Bending down she lifts the veil, presses his head upon her breast with her left hand, takes the cup* ORNELLA *offers and puts it to* ALIGI's *lips. A confusion of muffled voices rises from the people in the yard and down the path.*]

IONA DI MIDIA

Suscipe, Domine, servum tuum.
(Accept, O Lord, this thy servant.)
Kyrie eleison.

THE CROWD

Christe eleison, Kyrie eleison,
Miserere, Deus, miserere.

190

— Do you see, do you see his face?

This do we see upon earth, Jesus!

— Oh! Oh! Passion of the Saviour!

— But who is calling aloud? And wherefore?

— Be silent now! Hush, hush! Who is calling?

— The daughter of Jorio! The daughter of
Jorio, Mila di Codra!

— Great God, but this is a miracle!

— It is the daughter of Jorio coming.

— Good God! She is raised from the dead!

— Make room! Make room! Let her pass
by!

— Accursèd dog, are you yet living?

— Ah! Witch of Hell, is it you?

— She-dog! Harlot! Carrion!

— Back! Back! Make room! Let her pass!

— Come, she-thing, come! Make way!

— Let her pass through! Let her alone! In
the Lord's name!

[ALIGI *rises to his feet, his face uncovered.*
He looks toward the clamoring crowd, the

191

mother and sisters still near him. Impetu-
ously opening her way through the crowd,
MILA *appears.*

MILA DI CODRA

Mother of Aligi, sisters
Of Aligi, Bride and Kindred,
Standard-bearer of Wrong-Doing, and you,
All ye just people! Judge of God!
I am Mila di Codra.
I come to confess. Give me hearing.
The saint of the mountain has sent me.
I have come down from the mountain,
I am here to confess in public
Before all. Give me hearing.

IONA DI MIDIA

Silence! Be silent! Let her have leave
To speak, in the name of God, let her.
Confess yourself, Mila di Codra.
All the just people shall judge you.

MILA

Aligi, the beloved son of Lazaro,
Is innocent. He did not commit

THE SACRIFICE OF MILA DI CODRA.

Act III., Page 192.

Parricide.　But by me indeed was his father
Slain, by me was he killed with the axe.

ALIGI

Mila, God be witness that thou liest!

IONA

He has confessed it.　He is guilty.
But you too are guilty, guilty with him.

THE CROWD

To the fire with her!　To the fire with her!
　Now, Iona,
Give her to us, let us destroy her.
— To the brush heap with the sorceress,
Let them perish in the same hour together!
— No, no!　I said it was so.　He is innocent.
— He confessed it!　He confessed it!　The
　woman
Spurred him to do it.　But he struck the blow.
— Both of them guilty!　To the fire!　To the
　fire!

MILA

People of God! Give me hearing
And afterward punish me.
I am ready. For this did I come here.

IONA

Silence! All! Let her speak!

MILA

Aligi, dear son of Lazaro,
Is innocent. But he knows it not.

ALIGI

Mila, God be witness that thou liest.
Ornella (oh! forgive me that I dare to
Name you!) bear thou witness
That she is deceiving the good people.

MILA

He does not know. Aught of that hour
Is gone from his memory. He is bewitched.
I have upset his reason,
I have confused his memory.

194

I am the Sorcerer's daughter. There is no
Sorcery that I do not know well,
None that I cannot weave. Is there one
Of the kindred among you, that one
Who accused me in this very place,
The evening of Santo Giovanni,
When I entered here by that door before us?
Let her come forth and accuse me again!

LA CATALANA

I am that one. I am here.

MILA

Do you bear witness and tell for me
Of those whom I have caused to be ill,
Of those whom I have brought unto death,
Of those whom I have in suffering held.

LA CATALANA

Giovanna Cametra, I know.
And the poor soul of the Marane,
And Alfonso and Tillura, I know.
And that you do harm to every one.

MILA

Now have you heard this thing, all you good
  people,
What this servant of God hath well said and
  truly?
Here I confess.   The good saint of the
  mountain
Has touched to the quick my sorrowing con-
  science,
Here I confess and repent.   O permit not
The innocent blood to perish.
Punishment do I crave.   O punish me greatly!
To bring down ruin and to sunder
Dear ties and bring joys to destruction,
To take human lives on the day of the wedding
Did I come here to cross this threshold,
Of the fireplace there I made myself
The mistress, the hearth I bewitched,
The wine of hospitality I conjured,
Drink it I did not, but spilled it with sorceries.
The love of the son, the love of the father,
I turned into mutual hatred;
In the heart of the bride all joy strangled,

And by this my cunning, the tears
Of these young and innocent sisters
I bent to the aid of my wishes.
Tell me then, ye friends and kindred,
Tell me then, in the name of the Highest,
How great, how great is this my iniquity!

CHORUS OF THE KINDRED

It is true! It is true! All this has she done.
Thus glided she in, the wandering she-dog!
While yet Cinerella was pouring
Her handful of wheat on Vienda.
Very swiftly she did all her trickery,
By her evil wishes overthrowing
Very swiftly the young bridegroom.
And we all cried out against it.
But in vain was our crying. She had the trick
    of it.
It is true. Now only does she speak truly.
Praises to Him who this light giveth!

[ALIGI, *with bent head, his chin resting on
his breast, in the shadow of the veil, is intent
and in a terrible perturbation and contest of*

197

soul, the symptoms at the same time, appearing
in him of the effect of the potion.]

ALIGI

No, no, it is not true; she is deceiving
You, good people, do not heed her,
For this woman is deceiving you.
All of them here were all against her,
Heaping shame and hatred on her,
And I saw the silent angel
Stand behind her. With these eyes I saw him,
These mortal eyes that shall not witness
On this day the star of vesper.
I saw him gazing at me, weeping.
O Iona, it was a miracle,
A sign to show me her, God's dear one.

MILA

O Aligi, you poor shepherd!
Ignorant youth, and too believing!
That was the Apostate Angel!

[*They all cross themselves, except* ALIGI,
prevented from doing so by his fetters, and

ORNELLA *who, standing alone at one side of the porch, gazes intently on the voluntary victim.*]

Then appeared the Apostate Angel
(Pardon of God I must ever lack,
Nor of you, Aligi, be pardoned!)
He appeared your own two eyes to deceive.
It was the false and iniquitous angel.

MARIA CORA

I said it was so. At the time I said it.
It was a sacrilege then, I cried.

LA CINERELLA

And I said it, too, and cried out
When she dared call it the guardian angel
To watch over her. I cried out,
" She is blaspheming, she is blaspheming! "

MILA

Aligi, forgiveness from you, I know,
Cannot be, even if God forgive me.
But I must all my fraud uncover.

Ornella, oh! do not gaze upon me
As you gaze. I must stay alone!
Aligi, then when I came to the sheepstead,
Then, even, when you found me seated,
I was planning out your ruin.
And then you carved the block of walnut,
Ah, poor wretch, with your own chisel,
In the fallen angel's image!
(There it is, with the white cloth covered,
I feel it.) Ah! from dawn until evening
With secret art I wove spells upon you!
Remember them, do you not now of me?
How much love I bestowed upon you!
How much humility, in voice and demeanor —
Before your very face spells weaving?
Remember them, do you not now of me?
How pure we remained, how pure
I lay on your shepherd's pallet?
And how then? — how (did you not inquire?)
Such purity then, timidity, then,
In the sinning wayfarer
Whom the reapers of Norca
Had shamed as the shameless one

Before your mother? I was cunning,
Yea, cunning was I with my magic.
And did you not see me then gather
The chips from your angel and shavings,
And burn them, words muttering?
For the hour of blood I was making ready.
For of old against Lazaro
I nursed an old-time rancor.
You struck in your axe in the angel, —
O now must you heed me, God's people!
Then there came a great power upon me
To wield over him there now fettered.
It was close upon night in that ill-fated
Lodging. Lust-crazed then his father
Had seized me to drag toward the entrance,
When Aligi threw himself on us,
In order to save and defend me.
I brandished the axe then with swiftness.
In the darkness I struck him,
I struck him again. Yea, to death I felled
    him!
With the same stroke I cried, " You have
    killed him."

To the son I cried out, "You have killed
    him.
Killed him!" And great in me was my
    power.
A parricide with my cry I made him —
In his own soul enslaved unto my soul.
"I have killed him!" he answered, and swoon-
    ing,
He fell in the bloodshed, naught otherwise
    knowing.

[CANDIA, *with a frantic impulse, seizes with
both hands her son, become once more her own.
Then, detaching herself from him, with wilder
and threatening gestures, advances on her
enemy, but the daughters restrain her.*]

CHORUS OF KINDRED

Let her do it, let her, Ornella!
— Let her tear her heart! Let her eat
Her heart! Heart for heart!
Let her seize her and take her
And underfoot trample her.
— Let her crush in and shiver

Temple to temple and shell out her teeth.
Let her do it, let her, Ornella!
Unless she do this she will not win back
Her mind and her senses in health again.
— Iona, Iona, Aligi is innocent.
— Unshackle him! Unshackle him!
— Take off the veil! Give him back to us!
— The day is ours, the people do justice.
— The righteous people give judgment.
— Command that he now be set free.

[MILA *retreats near the covered angel,
looking toward* ALIGI, *who is already under
the influence of the potion.*]

THE CROWD

— Praises be to God! Glory be to God!
  Glory to the Father!
— From us is this infamy lifted.
— Not upon us rests this blood-stain.
— From our generation came forth
No parricide. To God be the glory!
— Lazaro was killed by the woman,
The stranger, di Codra dalle Farne.

—We have said and pronounced: he is in-
   nocent.
Aligi is innocent. Unbind him!
—Let him be free this very moment!
—Let him be given unto his mother!
—Iona, Iona, untie him! Untie him!
Unto us this day the Judge of Wrong-Doing
Over one head gave us full power.
—Take the head of the sorceress!
—To the fire, to the fire with the witch!
—To the brushheap with the sorceress!
—O Iona di Midia, heed the people!
Unbind the innocent! Up, Iona!
—To the brush heap with the daughter
Of Jorio, the daughter of Jorio!

MILA

Yes, yes, ye just people, yes, ye people
Of God! Take ye your vengeance on me!
And put ye in the fire to burn with me
The Apostate Angel, the false one, —
Let it feed the flames to burn me
And let it with me be consumed!

ALIGI

Oh! voice of promising, voice of deceit,
Utterly tear away from within me
All of the beauty that seemed to reign there,
Beauty so dear unto me! Stifle
Within my soul the memory of her!
Will that I have heard her voice never,
Rejoiced in it never! Smooth out within me
All of those furrows of loving
That opened in me, when my bosom
Was unto her words of deceiving
As unto the mountain that's channelled
With the streams of melting snow! Close up
      within me
The furrow of all that hope and aspiring
Wherein coursed the freshness and gladness
Of all of those days of deceiving!
Cancel within me all traces of her!
Will it that I have heard and believed never!
But if this is not to be given me, and I am
      the one
Who heard and believed and hoped greatly,
And if I adored an angel of evil,

Oh! then I pray that ye both my hands sever,
And hide me away in the sack of leather
(Oh! do not remove it, Leonardo),
And cast me into the whirling torrent,
To slumber there for years seven hundred,
To sleep in the depths there under the water;
In the pit of the river-bed, years seven hundred,
And never remember the day
When God lighted the light in my eyes!

ORNELLA

Mila, Mila, 't is the delirium,
The craze of the cup of forgetfulness
To console him he took from the mother.

THE CROWD

— Untie him, Iona, he is delirious.
— He has taken the wine potion.
— Let his mother lay him down on the settle.
— Let sleep come! Let him slumber!
— Let the good God give him slumber.

[IONA *gives the standard to another and comes to* ALIGI *to untie him.*]

ALIGI

Yes, for a little while free me, Iona,
So that I may lift my hand against her
(No, no, burn her not, for fire is beautiful!)
So that I call all the dead of my birthplace,
Those of years far away and forgotten,
Far, far away, far, far away,
Lying under the sod, fourscore fathom,
To curse her forever, to curse her!

MILA [*with a heart-rending cry*]

Aligi, Aligi, not you!
Oh! you cannot, you must not.

[*Freed from the manacles, the veil with-
drawn,* ALIGI *comes forward but falls back
unconscious in the arms of his mother, the older
sisters and the kindred gathering around him.*]

CHORUS OF KINDRED

You need not be frightened.   'T is the wine
only,
'T is the vertigo seizes him.
— Now the stupor falls upon him.

— Now slumber, deep slumber, o'erpowers
  him.
— Let him sleep, and may God give him
  peace!
— Let him lie down! Let him slumber!
— Vienda, Vienda, he is yours again.
— From the other world both will return now.
Laus Deo! Laus Deo! Gloria Patri!

[Iona *puts the manacles upon* Mila's
*wrists, who offers both arms and covers her
head with the black veil, then taking the standard of Wrong-Doing he pushes her toward the
crowd.*]

IONA

I give to you, just people,
Into your hands, Mila di Codra,
The daughter of Jorio, that one
Who does harm to every one.
Do you perform justice upon her,
And let her ashes be scattered.
O Lord, save thy people.
Kyrie eleison.

THE CROWD

Christe eleison! Kyrie eleison!
To the fire, to the flames with the daughter
Of Jorio! The daughter of Jorio!
And to the fire with the Apostate Angel!
To the brushheap with them! To hell-fire
    with them!

ORNELLA [*with full voice in majesty*]

Mila, Mila! My sister in Jesus,
I kiss your feet that bear you away!
Heaven is for thee!

MILA [*from within the crowd*]

The flame is beautiful! The flame is beautiful!

THE END